Exploring the Divine Library

by Richard Rowe

For permission, or serialization, condensation, adaptions, or for our catalog of other publications, write to: Ozark Mountain Publishing, Inc., P.O. Box 754, Huntsville, AR 72740, ATTN: Permissions Department

Library of Congress Cataloging-in-Publication Data
Exploring the Divine Library by Richard Rowe -1959-

Exploring the Divine Library explores projound insights by way of meditation, past-life regression, channeling information, remote viewing, dowsing, automatic writing, and astral projection.

1. Spriritual 2. Past-Live Regression 3. Meditation 4. Metaphysical
I. Rowe, Richard, 1959 II. Metaphysical III. Meditation IV. Title

Library of Congress Catalog Card Number: 2020939793
ISBN: 9781940265803

Cover Art and Layout: Victoria Cooper Art
Book set in: Times New Roman
Book Design: Summer Garr

Published by:

PO Box 754, Huntsville, AR 72740
800-935-0045 or 479-738-2348; fax 479-738-2448
WWW.OZARKMT.COM
Printed in the United States of America

Contents

Be patient toward all that is unsolved in your heart and try to love the questions themselves, like locked rooms and like books that are now written in a very foreign tongue. Do not now seek the answers, which cannot be given you because you would not be able to live them. And the point is, to live everything. Live the questions now. Perhaps you will then gradually, without noticing it, live along some distant day into the answer.

- Rainer Maria Rilke

Introduction

Living through a pulmonary embolism was a life-changing moment. The experience motivated me to ask a very simple question: why is there so much suffering in the world? That question launched me on an incredible spiritual journey.

After a great deal of research and exploration, I continued to ask questions leading me deeper down the metaphoric Alice in Wonderland's rabbit hole. I worked hard to pull back my veil of forgetfulness to answer my questions and search for insights that might ease the suffering of our present life experience. The more I worked at connecting beyond myself through meditation, regression, and astral projection, the more I found it easier to do so. Eventually, goose bumps rippled across my skin like ocean waves most of the time.

The role of my physical brain has become my translator. It collates, sorts, organizes, and assigns meaning to an inflow of images and information. Some may call this channeling, but I call it "focused intention" while listening to the silence without judging the information emerging within my mind. I continue to sketch the images I see with my mind's eye into two- dimensional diagrams and describe them.

This second book memorializes my continued journey and explores how anyone can learn to access information from what I refer to as the Divine Library. I study many topics in this book including energy flow, how to channel insights from spiritual realms, how to communicate telepathically with other consciousnesses anywhere in the multiverse, and how to create your own energetic inventions.

After Imagining the Unimaginable, referred to throughout this book as book one, was released, my mother read the book. It prompted her to openly talk about some of her personal spiritual experiences. She had kept those experiences to herself because it was hard for her to discuss such topics. She told me that my book had given her confidence to share her experiences.

One experience she shared occurred during the time of my grandmother's physical death. My mother was spending time at the bedside of my grandmother, who lay unconscious in a hospital bed and unable to communicate. My mother had heard from news reports that talking to a person in a coma could be beneficial. So she talked to my comatose grandmother during her visits.

As my grandmother's condition worsened, my mother spent more time with her.

During one such visit, my mother decided she would go through the physical motions of painting my grandmother's fingernails without actually using nail polish. My mother talked to her with each imaginary nail-painting motion as my grandmother remained unresponsive.

Suddenly, my mother's perspective changed.

At first, my mother felt disoriented but then realized she was gazing at the ceiling of the hospital room directly above my grandmother's bed. It made no sense to her. As my mother described it, she had somehow gone inside of my grandmother as though she became part of her, peering upward through my grandmother's eyes.

Then my mother's perspective changed a second time. She found herself standing in some unknown place directly in front of my grandmother. The two of them were having a conversation.

My mother described the conversation as follows: "Mother told me she had been around the world. She had visited a massive library and learned everything there was to learn. Mother insisted on telling me that only one word out of the entire library of information really mattered. It felt very important. That word was the most important thing to know about life. So I asked, 'what word?' Mother said the most important word of all is love. Love is what life is all about. It's really true."

My mother continued sharing her experience. "Right after Mother told me that, I found myself back in the chair along the side of her bed. Mother passed shortly afterward."

After my mother's experience, she held on to those memories of my grandmother, but kept the details to herself. Now she was eager to share it and allow me to write about it.

It was an incredible feeling listening to my mother open up.

Perhaps it is the right time to start talking openly to each other about our spiritual experiences without fear of reprisal or being defined as "crazy." Maybe we can integrate the subject matter of life after death into the mainstream?

I hope others will feel the same and share their experiences with their family and close friends. I believe sharing our personal stories will help us to realize just how much we are all connected and how beautiful life can be.

I felt blessed to have shared that moment with my mother, but there was another part of our discussion I want to mention. When I told my mother about writing this second book, she asked me what the book was about. I told her I was still adding material to the manuscript, but the first part of the book is all about accessing information from what I describe as the "Divine Library."

We both smiled. Maybe the Divine Library I discuss in this book is that same library my grandmother had visited before she passed on?

This second book asks many new questions, including the following: Where does the information come from for my ideas and inventions? Where does the information come from for life reviews, soul records, etc.? Could there be an external source of information such as the Akashic Records referred to by spiritual teachers and others, which is said to contain every lifetime experience of every soul? Can I apply the same approach I use to invent physical systems to create energetic inventions?

From ancient times to the present day, many names have been used to refer to information existing somewhere beyond our three-dimensional universe. These names include Akashic Field, Heavenly Library, the Book of Life, Hall of Two Truths, Library of Light, Cosmic Mind, the Matrix, Universal Library, Collective Subconscious, Holographic Library, and others.

For purposes of this book, I refer to the superset of spiritual information stored beyond our third dimension as the Divine Library and integrate data from the Divine Library into my discovery process to search for spiritual insights.

To facilitate the understanding of a Divine Library existing in higher dimensions, I develop a toolset of functional building blocks. I describe how life experiences might be recorded and offer suggestions on how to access the library to answer my deeper questions about life.

By examining new questions using information gleaned from the library, I hope to provide a unique perspective of spiritual realms, forming a broader understanding of consciousness and ultimately enhancing our daily lives by applying lessons learned.

I apply lessons learned to demonstrate how anyone can receive answers from the library related to a wide range of topics, including life purpose, spiritual connection, telepathic communication, and living a joyful life.

I go on to ask more questions. How is information stored for the life review process discussed in book one? How do telepathy, remote viewing, out-of-body experiences, and dowsing work? Where do we go when we have these experiences? Why do so many believe we are in a holographic universe?

My questions went deeper still. As I searched for an understanding about the nature of consciousness, working as a cocreator, and the mechanisms within higher dimensions. These questions are not intended to create some new belief system or challenge any existing ones. Rather, I aim to uncover insights that can be used to help readers develop a basic understanding of higher dimensions.

While I continue to ask big questions and seek understanding, I recognize answers are not my only purpose for asking these questions. Instead, spiritual growth, the process of discovery, and a sincere desire to comprehend spiritual realms from my perspective as a lifelong inventor are what motivate me.

As part of the research for this book, I learned about dowsing and attended a remote viewing master class taught by Angela Smith, PhD.

My perspective of consciousness continued to expand. Could I connect remotely to access information using remote viewing protocols? Is it possible to use a process similar to remote viewing protocols for basic telepathy?

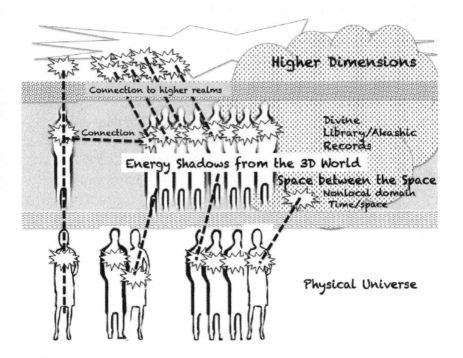

As I reflected on reports of near-death experiencers (NDErs) who experience an energetic reflection of Earth then move toward a light or tunnel, I speculated that a dimensional buffer zone must exist between our third dimension and the fourth dimension. This buffer zone can be envisioned as an in-between realm souls pass through during an NDE and where out-of-body experiencers (OBErs) experience astral projections.

This spiritual realm could be the same place where information from a Divine Library is accessed, where telepathy occurs, where channeling occurs, and so on. I further reasoned that if I could connect telepathically with people on Earth, I should be able to communicate with other consciousnesses anywhere in the multiverse.

The questions I explored and the insights that emerged led me to a deeper understanding of the importance of focused intent, quieting one's conscious mind, meditation, prayer, and connection. In later chapters, I explore what is behind the idea that our present reality is an illusion and how we can create a personalized version of reality. I develop an approach to understand challenging concepts and show readers how anyone can create energetic inventions and apply them to enhance their life experience.

Irrespective of my approach to answering questions in this book, I challenge you to decide what is meaningful to you. Debate my perspective and proposed solutions from afar. Talk about your ideas and experiences. Read the reference sources I include in the back of the book. Form your own opinions. Challenge my interpretations to form new opinions. Pick and choose what resonates for your spiritual expedition then continue on with your journey.

Notwithstanding language differences or positions on the metaphoric spiritual elephant described in book one, I am confident my spiritual discovery as articulated in this book will aid readers on their spiritual journey.

I hope the presented research, ideas, and insights motivate us all to collectively shape our physical world into a world we have always hoped and dreamed it could be, a world molded in such a way where suffering does not limit our growth potential nor extend the number of lifetimes required to learn the life lessons we wish to learn.

Thank you for joining me on my spiritual journey.

Chapter 1
The Journey Continues

This spiritual journey continues to be full of wonder, excitement, and amazing experiences. I marvel at the beauty of it all. We are multidimensional creatures who have chosen to experience this particular dimension with all of its challenges. I have come to believe such extremes of joy and suffering are learning opportunities. These learning opportunities are why we have incarnated on this world.

The focus of my exploration continues to be driven by questions that deeply resonate with me. I research a variety of first-hand experiences and my own experiences to search for insights. This process is very similar to the approach I have used throughout my career as an inventor to invent, describe, and document systems systematically.

I push harder to search for more profound insights to brighten this life experience by way of meditation, regression, channeling information, and psychic (psi) techniques. I explored regression, remote viewing, dowsing, channeling, automatic writing, and astral projection. The more I worked at allowing my consciousness to explore other dimensions, the easier it became to reach altered states of consciousness to search for insights to my questions.

My exploration eventually led me to the question: "what is consciousness?"

While many have explored the consciousness question, I examine the consciousness question from the perspective of an inventor searching for answers and a comprehensible understanding.

To explore my questions in this second book, I use a similar approach as used in book one. Additionally, I include the application of many different methods: guided hypnosis, regressions, between-life recollections, self-hypnosis, meditation, remote viewing, dowsing, out- of-body experiences, channeling, telepathy, and others.

My research and experiences have led me to believe we are multidimensional beings and exist in all dimensions simultaneously. To experience existence, we focus our intention to experience a particular realm like we are doing right now in this three-dimensional (3D) physical world.

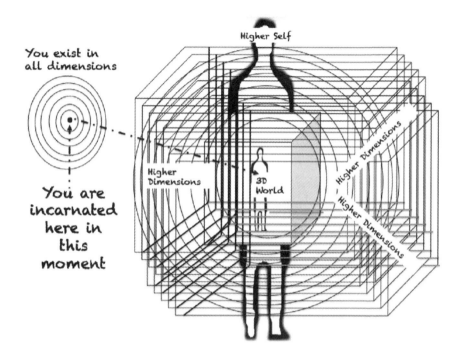

Using a variety of approaches, I allow my consciousness to explore remote places or topics of interest and open myself up to that experience. Additionally, I often silence my ego and study past-life lessons to understand how best to handle a particular situation in my present life or open myself up to new ideas and a flow of information.

Many have written and discussed the notion that we create our universe, but I never really understood it until now. The idea sounded too large and abstract for me to understand and apply to my life. The concept of "creating my universe" felt beyond my grasp.

As I worked hard to understand and receive answers to my

questions, I discovered the limitations of our earthly languages. Yet I also found each of us has the power to manifest that which we truly need in this lifetime. Not in a way where I snap my fingers and a pile of money shows up, but rather where I ask the universe for guidance and focus my awareness on my life choices and positive experiences that will facilitate my soul growth and physical well-being.

Finding balance and reacting to stressful situations with love rather than a demanding Ego is what I strive to do. Granted, even with a greater understanding about the nature of "who I am" and "why I am here" I can still get overwhelmed by the demands of the "Ego" part of my "Self."

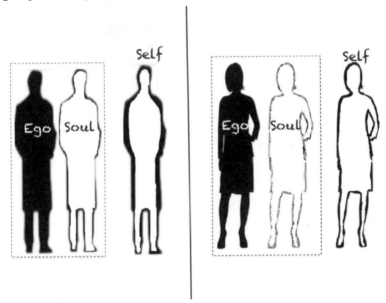

I wondered if a book two should ask questions about the dynamics of life, the concept of using energy to heal, or the nature of time. What helpful insights can I offer others to optimize their life experience? Exploration, examination, and extrapolation are what explorers of knowledge have always done. It is what seekers of understanding do. It is what engineers and inventors do. It is what I do!

I sent out my inquiry with a loving prayer asking for divine guidance on the topics for a second book. What sort of information do I need now for my spiritual journey? What information will aid readers of my books on their spiritual journeys?

I waited and listened to the silence without preconceived answers floating around in my mind. I told myself not to force an answer or make assumptions. Worse case, maybe there was no need for a second book? I did not want to write anything without an inspired theme to explore or an important message to present. I stayed open and willing to receive divine guidance.

After some weeks, the answer came.

To my amazement, the answer arrived in the backseat of an Uber ride after a patent training session with a client. Being new to using services like Lyft and Uber, I was excited about using the service, and it lived up to my expectations. I found the drivers to be very friendly and excited about sharing their thoughts with me about the service. My inventor curiosity listened attentively to the stories.

Each driver shared similar experiences about the benefits of working independently: work-hour flexibility, supporting their family, paying for school tuition, etc. Of course, the drivers asked me questions about why I was in town, where I was from, and so on.

On my last ride back to the airport, I met a gentleman who had recently become an Uber driver. He spoke very little English, but we managed to exchange pleasantries. He was very polite and friendly.

I asked him what he did when he was not driving. He told me he was a pastor at a small struggling church and the money he made driving would be used to help his congregation. Mind you, he was not asking for a donation or expecting anything from me. He was merely answering the question I had asked him.

I asked more questions, and he went on to tell me about the people his church supported. Before long, I asked him to tell me about the most important lesson he had learned as a pastor.

The gentleman paused, considering my question, and then responded with a grin I saw in his rearview mirror, "People just want to know they have a purpose."

It was as if a lightbulb flashed on. I knew in that instant his answer was important for me to explore deeper. I interpreted the response to mean people want to feel their life is relevant and meaningful.

As I reflected on his response later, I realized that most people eventually ask follow-up questions: Why am I here? Is there a specific reason I am alive? If so, what is it?

After the business trip, I began a deeper dive into the notion of life purpose. What is a life purpose? Do we have more than one life purpose? Can our life purpose change in the middle of our lifetime?

From my research into NDEs, I learned some near-death experiencers recall a discussion about their life purpose with spiritual entities during their out-of-body experience (OBE) in spiritual realms.

Some NDErs are told they still have important tasks to do and must return to their body. Upon returning to their physical body, many NDErs cannot remember the details about what they had been told. These NDErs report a strong feeling in their gut suggesting their life purpose is important.

Some believe they cannot remember because it is not the right earthly time and "knowing" before it is time may disrupt the unfolding of life events.

Another essential aspect of NDEs I wondered about related to the life review process. NDErs talk about experiencing a full lifetime playback while they are out of their body. During this lifetime playback, the NDEr learns what is most important in their life. They confirm their life has meaning—it matters. The experience changes their perspective about what matters in their life when they return to the body.

I found the lifetime playback process to be fascinating and wondered how such a heavenly system functioned given that a playback implies storage coupled with the ability to access the stored information.

How and where does one's life experience get stored? How is it possible? How can a full lifetime be played back? Could the life playback relate to the spiritual library some people talk about while under deep hypnosis?

I discovered numerous references to a "Heavenly Library" and "soul books" mentioned by subjects under deep hypnosis who experience past-life regressions and in-between life regressions. Some people under deep hypnosis describe entering a library or great hall. They often receive a book with relevant personal information about the lives that particular soul had lived and the soul's overall journey.

This library resonated with me after the additional insights I had gained during my past- life regressions and between-life hypnotherapy sessions. I wondered if the library could be used to search for information on life purpose and provide answers to my other questions similar to a Dewey Decimal System in a traditional brick-and-mortar library or perhaps like an Internet search engine.

Does the library include information about what might be holding someone back from achieving life purpose? Can this library be accessed by anyone searching for an answer to any question? Is access to the library soul specific?

The questions kept coming.

How does access to information in the library work? Is each soul only allowed to obtain their personal information or can they access other souls' information? Does the library include details about the nature of physical life and our universe? Is this where creative ideas come from "out of the blue?"

I soon discovered a reference source referred to by numerous names since the beginning of human history including the Book of Life, Akashic Records, and the other names mentioned earlier in the introduction. This reference source is said to be a compilation of all events, thoughts, dreams, emotions, and words that have ever occurred in our physical realm in the past, present, and future, where future includes forthcoming events and probable future scenarios based on the assertion of free will.

For purposes of this book, I combine the information about a Heavenly Library reported by hypnotherapists such as Michael Newton, Dolores Cannon, Scott Fitzgerald De Tamble, and many others with the soul-oriented information from the Akashic Records or Book of Life. This superset of heavenly information is what I describe as the Divine Library.

I apply a systematic process using my inventor perspective with focused intention and an open mind to gain a deeper understanding of higher dimensions through the filter of my insights and experience.

Aspects of the Divine Library are extrapolated and shaped into a toolset comprised of building blocks to help me understand a theoretical structure to illustrate how soul lifetime information can be stored, accessed, and interpreted.

I don't challenge or tell others what they should or shouldn't believe. My journey is not intended to debate traditional or nontraditional religious, new age, mystical, metaphysical, or any other beliefs for that matter. It is not meant to disrespect the beliefs or traditions of others. Nor is it my intention to disrespect the spiritual information source often referred to as the Akashic Records by referencing it as a subset of information stored in what I call the Divine Library.

I am just one person on a personal spiritual journey transforming insights into diagrams while using words to describe ideas, dreams, thoughts, and questions that resonate with me.

Together we share the physical world at this divinely orchestrated moment in time. We are, so to say, in this lifetime together—all of us. As we continue forward on this spiritual journey, consider the immortal words of Winston Churchill, "Success is not final, failure is not fatal: it is the courage to continue that counts."

Chapter 2
The Divine Library

I first became aware of the existence of a divine source of the soul's recorded lifetime information when I studied past-life and between-life hypnotherapy. Often subjects under deep hypnosis describe a library with soul books that contain a recording of the soul's lifetime experiences.

Certified master trainer and hypnotherapist Scott Fitzgerald De Tamble learned about the library from his subjects under deep hypnosis. He describes the library as follows:

"Spirit world libraries are described by clients as incredibly vast halls in which information is stored in the form of books, scrolls, or even on watchable video screens. Souls are often directed to a library by their spirit guides in order to learn about a specific issue of importance . . . People generally visit the library to gather data on their own past lives. But as in any library, other information is available, including advanced works on science, history, the arts, etc. Library Archivists are usually present to assist souls with locating or viewing resources" (De Tamble 2018).

For more detailed information about the library from hypnotherapy sessions and information gleaned from his subjects, refer to my interview with certified master trainer and hypnotherapist Scott Fitzgerald De Tamble in Appendix A.

The notion of a Divine Library became real to me when I experienced my past-life regressions and hypnotherapy. This prompted new questions about the nature of such a divine resource. I wanted to understand this library better, maybe even visualize it.

How did I experience my past lives in more detail than a dream? How did the regression facilitate playback such that I could experience important parts of those lives? Is there a heavenly database filled with information that I can reference? Does general information exist about the nature of existence in this spiritual database?

To incorporate a Divine Library as a source of recorded soul lifetimes and other information as a reference resource for this book, the library must be understandable.

Before attempting to use such a library to access information, I needed to understand the library's structure, content, and functionality. I speculated understanding would help me grasp the information available from the library and how to access it. But how can I describe a source of information that exists in a higher dimension from the limited perspective of my three- dimensional (3D) worldview?

As I broadened my exploration, I found many other similar divine reference sources throughout human history. While the names of the reference sources were different, the content sounded similar to content in the library as reported by subjects under deep hypnosis.

I concluded that each of these references must be the same library from different perspectives. To avoid confusion with other library perspectives and to be consistent with the spiritual library referenced during past-life regressions, and between-life regressions, I assigned the spiritual resource a generic name, the Divine Library.

Next, I began to model the Divine Library to describe it just as I would do to comprehend any complex system. Then I encountered my first challenge.

Given such a divine resource must have both a storage capability of source information and a mechanism to receive it, how could such a storage system in a higher dimension be described using our simple earthly languages?

With storage of lifetime experience and other information in a multidimensional spiritual data cloud, I realized I needed to describe the library in sketches to help me illustrate how it might work.

I started the process by sketching the figure below to depict how energy fluctuations and vibrations could be shaped into life experiences moments, linked, and stored inside the Divine Library.

I quickly realized even if language challenges are resolved entirely, readers might still disagree about word meaning and context. At best, it seems our languages, such as English, might be able to describe only a three-dimensional cross-section of the Divine Library existing in a higher dimension.

To further understand the idea of a three-dimensional cross-section, recall the two- dimensional being living in a two-dimensional world described in the book entitled, Flatland: A Romance of Many Dimensions, written in 1884 by Edwin A. Abbott (who also wrote under the pseudonym A Square).

The two-dimensional line being named Square attempts to describe a three-dimensional being called "Sphere" who lives in a three-dimensional world. In the example I presented in book one, Square is only able to view a part, or cross-section, of Sphere. That is, Sphere reveals itself to Square in the form of a line that grows and shrinks as Sphere moves in front of Square. In other words, all

Square sees is a two-dimensional cross-section of Sphere.

Using the Flatland analogy, I realized that all I could hope to visualize and comprehend are the basics of a library's function and operation. So how does it work? Could higher- dimensional information stored in a Divine Library utilize fundamental elements grouped to record a soul's life experience?

Perhaps the information in the Divine Library is comprised of collections of emotions, feelings, frequency, harmonics, light, amplitude, intensity, and billions of colors.

Given I cannot fully comprehend higher dimensions, I applied what I already knew by way of data-processing analogy in an attempt to describe and interpret the information stored in the Divine Library.

By analyzing information in the library, I decided I could develop a basic understanding of how such a Divine Library worked and, more generally, how it could help me develop an understanding about data repository functionality in higher-dimensional realms.

Recall from this book's introduction that information stored in the Divine Library is a compilation of every energy fluctuation and vibration, all events, thoughts, emotions, words that have ever occurred in the past, present, and future in our three-dimensional universe.

One possible analogy to help visualize how such a massive amount of complex data can be recorded in higher dimensions is by way of a hologram data storage system used to store a light field such as a 3D photograph. The 3D scene is captured by a device and stored in two dimensions. When playback of the scene occurs, the 2D recording displays a projection of the original 3D scene without needing any special glasses.

The authors of the article "Review of Three-Dimensional Holographic Imaging by Multiple-Viewpoint-Projection Based Methods" write, "For visualization purposes, the holographically recorded 3D image can be easily reconstructed optically (for example, by illuminating the hologram with a coherent light)" (Shaked et al. 2009).

Of course, this analogy does not consider recording every energy fluctuation and vibration comprising such things as all events, thoughts, emotions, and words occurring during a soul's incarnated lifetime. But the analogy does provide an example of how a recording of three- dimensional data can be recorded and played back to recreate a recorded 3D scene.

Expanding on the hologram analogy, the stream of raw energy fluctuations and vibrations from our 3D universe could be recorded in higher dimensions as energy, vibration, light, and sound, allowing a soul's lifetime to be played back. Further, the stored information would enable the soul to replay the recording from every recorded 3D perspective just as NDErs have reported during life reviews. It is also consistent with many past-life regressions reported by Newton, Cannon, Tomlinson, De Tamble, and others.

Since a Divine Library must be able to collect and store a continuous stream of energy fluctuations and vibrations occurring throughout a soul's incarnated lifetime, it is convenient to organize the massive data stream into understandable pieces specifically associated with a soul's lifetime.

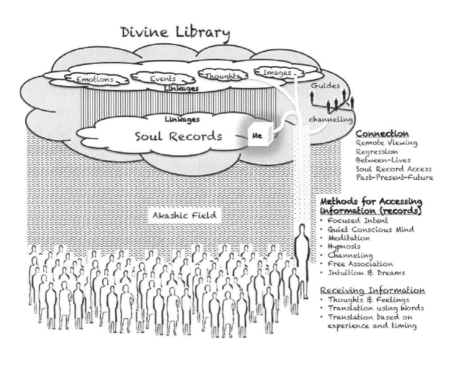

The above illustration reflects a big picture perspective of the Divine Library. By breaking down these details, I can start to understand how a higher-dimension data repository works.

Organizing the Stream

For the data stream to contain a particular soul's lifetime point of view (POV) and be organized for future access, it is essential to arrange the information into manageable pieces. For example, Earth-orbiting satellites transmit what is referred to as telemetry to a ground station where the ground station collects and interprets the information.

The manageable pieces are diced and sliced to store everything available and make playback possible. For purposes of this book, these pieces of data will be given the name "moments."

To further aid in the visualization process, a single moment will be defined as a fundamental component of the information stream relating to a single soul's lifetime experience point of view.

For example, when an incarnated soul tosses a pebble into a lake that results in a splash while a second soul observes the scene, the scene is recorded from multiple points of view. There is the incarnated soul's point of view, experiencing the tossing of a pebble and watching what happens when it hits the water. An additional second soul's point of view occurs, watching as the first soul tosses the stone through the air into the lake. Then there may be a third point of view from above the scene capturing a third-person perspective of the moments during the entire event.

The third-person perspective provides an impersonal viewpoint possibly consisting of one's "higher self" or the point of view of helpful spiritual entities such as Spirit Guides.

Irrespective of the source of the third-person perspective point of view, the perspective is often talked about by NDErs. This viewpoint occurs when the NDEr views their body and the death scene from above, or from a corner of a hospital room as emergency room personnel work on their body.

I experienced this point of view during my very first regression when I watched two people in ancient Egypt working on my lifeless body.

Moments

With a single moment defined as a fundamental component of the divine information stream, it is helpful to give this essential element context by exploring the next question: what is a moment? Most of us tend to take time for granted in our lives. I can peer at a digital clock in my three-dimensional world and imagine a moment by watching the seconds changing on the clock. For convenience purposes, I can relate a moment to a second.

A moment then becomes defined as a time interval of one second within which everything in that moment is recorded in the Divine Library including energy, vibration, events, thoughts, emotions, words, semantics, syntax, point of view, and any other essential elementary information.

From a big picture perspective, this means everything that has occurred in a single second anywhere in this universe is stored. Again, I am using seconds only to help me understand how raw information could be stored.

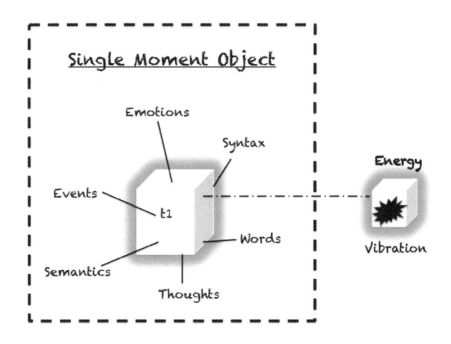

To visualize this idea of using a second to represent a moment think about how a webcam or mobile phone recording works. When I use my mobile phone to record and store a video scene, it collects video and audio, second by second, from the mobile phone's point of view. For the mobile phone, a second is defined as a moment of a video image and the associated sound, allowing the video to be paused, viewed, and replayed.

When I initiate playback of what has been stored by mobile phone, I watch a series of seconds or moments play out in what appears to me as a replay of the recorded scene.

I can pause the mobile phone playback and stop the video at any given second. Then I select play again to allow the video to continue. Similarly, the Divine Library must store the experience of every individual soul taking part in the scene as described above from their point of view.

Recall the reports from many NDErs who experience a life playback during their NDE that included various life experience events from their point of view as well as those events experienced from other incarnated souls' POVs who had shared the event.

Dr. Kenneth Ring's book, Lessons from the Light: What We Can Learn from the Near- Death Experience, includes a chapter on NDE life reviews. Ring's and Valarino's research includes NDErs who experienced a life review during their NDE where they were simultaneously the participant and an observer of it (Ring and Valarino 1998, 154).

In The Handbook of Near-Death Experiences, the researchers report, "memories revived during NDEs are frequently described as being 'many' or as an instantaneous 'panoramic' review of the person's entire life" (Holden, Greyson, and James 2009, 229).

In his book, Exploring the Eternal Soul, author and psychotherapist Andy Tomlinson writes about a frequently reported library life review setting containing life books that "come alive . . . like a little video inside the book that plays back certain scenes" (Tomlinson 2007, 62– 63).

For such a life experience playback to occur, where every moment is re-experienced by a soul from many points of view, it is logical to conclude a Divine Library must exist, and the stream of energy fluctuations and vibrations must be organized sufficiently to facilitate such a playback of a soul's incarnated lifetime.

To further organize the information associated with a soul's life experience into events, sequences of events can be said to comprise many connected moments over a number of seconds: $t = t1, t2, t3, t4, t5, t6, t7 \ldots tn$.

What if the unit of time for a moment is smaller than a second? It is easy to imagine just by referencing sporting events where milliseconds differentiate winners from losers.

Or maybe moments are defined at the atomic level? Could moments use a measure of time at the quantum or vibration level? Could moments comprise the recording of every energy fluctuation and vibration in the form of an energetic hologram? Could the universe's raw information be stored in an information framework structure, allowing playback from specific points of view?

Laszlo writes about the Akashic Field, or A-field, in his book, Science and the Akashic Field, "Generations after generations of humans left their holographic traces in the A-field, and the information in these holograms is available to read out" (Laszlo 2004, 115).

In the book, Akashic Records: Collective Keepers of Divine Expression, author Lumari writes, "The universe is an open system, which has specific vibratory criteria for access to certain wisdoms and experiences" (Lumari 2003, 23).

For purposes of my research and personal understanding, I decided to keep my model of the Divine Library as simple as possible by referring to everything that occurs in an Earth second as a single moment. Then I reference a sequence of moments during a soul's life experience as a life experience event.

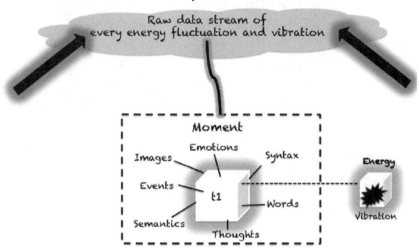

Thus the soul's life experience moment stored in the Divine Library consists of pieces of the raw stream of energy fluctuations and vibrations explicitly associated with the soul's lifetime experience. These energy fluctuations and vibrations are captured moment by moment during a soul's incarnation and include everything (thoughts, emotions, events, words, semantics, essential information, etc.) associated with the soul's experience from all points of view.

While this approach may seem to oversimplify or mechanize the stream of energy fluctuations and vibrations occurring in the universe, it is only used to help me imagine how a single moment can be experienced by the soul during a life review playback.

In the following diagram, t1 through tn represent moments in my lifetime. I use cloud diagrams as a reference since the recorded moment is far more than a freeze frame second of a mobile phone video, given that a moment symbolizes everything that can occur in a moment, including emotions, thoughts, and so on.

The first moment is labeled t1, then other moments, t2, t3 . . . tn, are linked together to form a sequence of moments. For example, t1 through tn may relate to a short playback of a single event that had occurred during my lifetime.

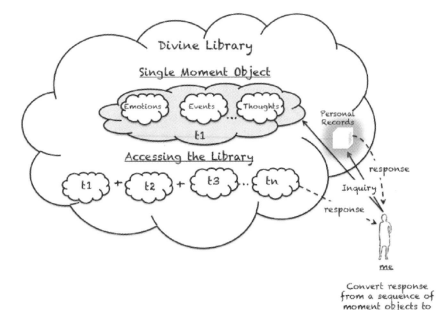

For convenience purposes, it is easier to represent these moments as blocks given these moments will be combined and grouped together later in this chapter. The blocks are merely meant to be symbolic of all the thoughts, emotions, etc., that occurred during a lifetime event from all points of view. The heavenly information related to the soul's lifetime experience span many moments, such as the example shown below.

The following diagrams assist me with the visualization of a soul's stored lifetime moments. I can imagine how these moments could be replayed and communicated from the Divine Library to the soul.

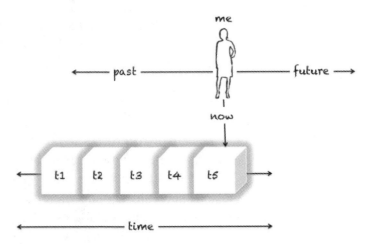

Sequence of Moment Objects

For lifetime events to be accessed and played back by a soul for study purposes or during a life review, soul-oriented moments are linked together into sequences. For example: t1, t2, t3, t4, t5 . . . tn. These soul-oriented sequences of moments represent the recordings of the soul's life experience events.

Sequences can be further segmented and categorized into critical events and groupings of sequences associated with significant turning points or major events in the soul's life. For example, life-changing emotional events may include many thousands of different sequences throughout one's life experience.

The exact number of sequences or categories is not important. This approach simply illustrates the ability for souls, Spirit Guides, and other spiritual entities to identify and retrieve events from a soul's lifetime for reference and study purposes. Additionally, when a first soul's life event is linked to a second soul's life event, that particular life event can be experienced by the soul from multiple points of view. As suggested earlier, the two points of view include the soul's point of view and another soul's point of view who shared the experience.

Content and Structure

Starting with the content aspect of the Divine Library and incorporating the discussion from book one related to an incarnated lifetime, the library must include a recording of every moment of the soul's lifetime experience (from birth to death) and every lifetime experienced by the soul.

In the figure below, item 1 represents the Divine Library where everything that has ever occurred is recorded as moments. From an individual soul perspective, recorded moments include every moment of a soul's incarnated life experience from birth, item 2, throughout his or her lifetime in physical form, items 3 and 4, until eventually returning to spiritual realms as shown in item 5.

From my experience with earthly databases, storage of ancillary events and logging of status information provide additional context for stored data. It makes sense to conclude contextual data associated with a soul's lifetime would also be recorded within the Divine Library.

Contextual information includes such data as item 6, whispers from Spirit Guides, and item 7, associated with assistance given to the incarnated soul by his or her Spirit Guides in the form of signs, whispers, or nudges.

The Spirit Guide assistance is then stored with the soul's records to enhance the recording, providing context related to crucial events that occurred during a soul's incarnated lifetime.

For example, Spirit Guides may whisper suggestions or hints that prompt an incarnated soul to assert free will to decide to take, or not take, a particular action. The Spirit Guidewhispers and the free will actions asserted by the incarnated soul are recorded together in the library to assist the soul's learning process by way of later review and study.

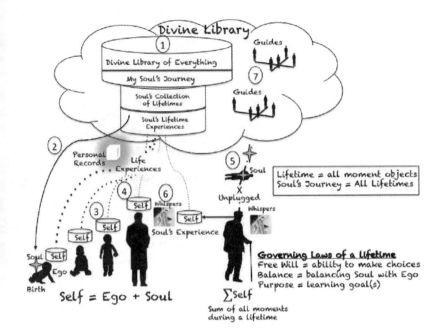

Content

With a Divine Library framework of moments established, it becomes meaningful to further describe possible categories of moments, Spirit Guide information, and other ancillary data. As shown in the figure below, the stored information is organized into example categories that include soul specific, soul group, and general physical world parameters.

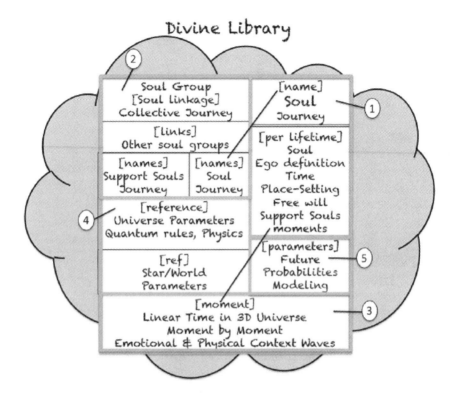

For example, item 1 reflects the framework of a soul's journey while item 2 represents information related to a group of souls with which the soul may be a member. Item 3 includes every moment associated with the soul's journey over the course of all its lifetimes. Item 4 includes the framework, parameters, and physical world constructs related to incarnation options for souls.

As a soul moves through many lifetime experiences, there may be learning setbacks or advancements as represented in the figure below.

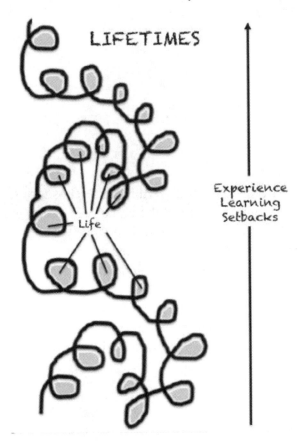

Instead of a straight line of lifetimes, there may be multiple lifetimes needed in order to learn a specific lesson or achieve a particular purpose. Growth may simply mean gaining the desired experience before moving on to new lessons.

Specific lifetimes of moment objects, represented by the shaded areas, are linked together and stored in the Divine Library. Other information can also be stored with each lifetime such as categories of information relating to a particular soul's life purpose, learning goals, lessons learned, lessons to be learned, lingering issues, soul group goals, life purpose, the physical world's life-cycle criteria, constructs, and fundamental lifetime features.

Given the massive amount of information stored in support of the soul's training, a new question arises: How can the Divine Library be accessed druing a soul's incarnated lifetime?

Chapter 3
Access

To access information in our earthly data repositories, commonly described as cloud storage or "the cloud," an action is required to initiate a request for information from a repository. Typical database queries are processed and the requested information is output to the requestor. The process of inquiry and response in its basic form is fundamental for accessing information.

To understand how this process might work for the Divine Library, I extrapolate the logic associated with earthly databases and "cloud storage" as an analogy to describe the functionality of the Divine Library.

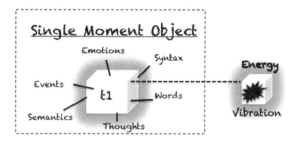

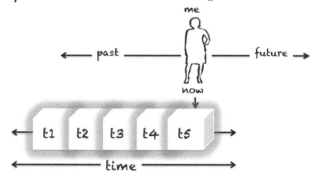

As discussed in the last chapter, single moments are collected and stored in the Divine Library during a soul's life as sequences of moments related to life events. Once saved, all the sequences form a soul's lifetime experience. Each lifetime experience is stored in a unique soul life book within the collection of all soul life books in the Divine Library.

For readers who do not understand how earthly databases and repositories work, the process is much like an Internet search where a user uses a web browser to access a search engine to search for website links on a particular topic. The user types in keywords into the search tool that describes the information of interest to the user. The user's request then searches massive data repositories referred to as "the cloud."

The search tool formats the data it collects from the data repository and displays it to the user in his or her web browser in the form of a list of website links relating to the information of interest to the user. With experience, most Internet users learn how to select the best keywords for their query to receive an optimal list of website addresses.

For purposes of describing a Divine Library, I imagine the process of accessing information from the Divine Library starts by a request for information from the soul. The Divine Library initiates a search and collects the desired moment sequences. Finally, a response is sent from the Divine Library to the requesting soul with the desired information.

Requesting Information

In the figure below, the soul makes an inquiry to the Divine Library by way of a specific request or question. To send out an inquiry, the request should take the form of a thought or verbal request with clear intention.

This raises a new question given we have countless thoughts every day. How can a single thought be defined as a request to receive information from the Divine Library?

The thought, or verbal request, we send to the Divine Library must be as specific as possible and sent with loving emotion and an open mind. This idea prompted me to wonder about the types of requests I might make to the Divine Library.

For example, thinking in terms of math and music savants I tried an experiment that involved learning something new such as a musical instrument.

Of course, after experimenting with this approach I found the request to learn the musical instrument did not result in me knowing how to play the instrument. This is not to say a similar request is impossible, but there appears to be more to making requests for information from the Divine Library than simply asking for something I want. Spiritual teacher and writer Gabrielle Orr writes in her book, Akashic Records, "The Akashic Records are a medium for consciousness development" (Orr 2013, 31).

Maybe savants simply remember prior life experiences and the associated muscle memory learned over many lifetimes?

After trial and error, I came to understand Orr's point about consciousness development. I discovered that my requests worked the best for me when they were associated with a genuine need.

To start the process as shown in the figure below, a calm mind or meditation with focused intent without the distraction of my Ego is essential to the process. Recall the reference I use in book one: the Self is the union of the immortal soul and the current-life human Ego.

"Let's define me as the integration of two essential parts. One part of me is my physical existence. Some call this my mind. I label this as Ego, not to be confused with the Freudian version of ego. This 'me' version of Ego (or body) is composed of a brain, hands, feet, eyes, ears, etc., and the physical instincts required for survival, including breathing, desire for pleasure, compulsion to reproduce, avoidance of pain, desire for food and drink, etc. The second part of me is my unique consciousness. Some call this my loving heart, associated with 'me' that exists beyond my skin boundary. From the context of the near-death experience, I label this 'me' version of consciousness to be my soul, composed of my true essence with higher level emotions, including empathy for others, love, forgiveness, and other emotions beyond the instincts required for survival in the physical world" (Rowe, Imagining the Unimaginable).

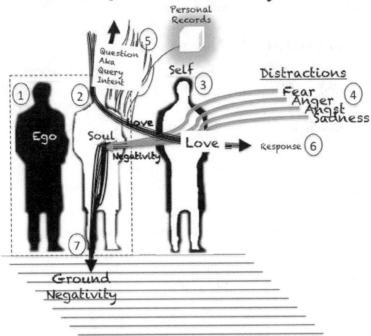

Connecting to the Divine Library

Breaking this down further: my ego (item 1) can disrupt my self's (item 3) ability to send requests (item 5) and receive responses (item 6) via my soul (item 2) by tainting my requests with (item 4) fear, anger, angst, and sadness. This interference comes from our conscious mind, which is connecting our physical body to the world around us. We must quiet that part of our Self to allow our soul, or consciousness, to gain access to spiritual realms.

From my experiments, it seems the way to avoid the scenario of my ego disrupting my self's requests, requires me to focus on sending out my requests with love and grounding negative energy (item 7) using meditation, focused intent, or prayer. Only after I put myself into this focused state of mind while shutting out the world around me do I have a chance of fully connecting beyond my Self to receive the desired information.

In her book, Sound Health, Sound Wealth: The Biology of Hope and Manifestation, author Luanne Oakes, PhD, says providing detail by writing, speaking aloud, sending out emotion, and envisioning using all parts of the body and mind is the way to communicate with the Universe (Oakes 2006, 59).

Connecting to the Divine Library

If people under deep hypnosis can access a spiritual library, I concluded that I should be able to access the library by quieting my mind. I worked out a process for accessing the Divine Library summarized in the following steps:

1. Trust the information you are seeking exists. Be open-minded to the idea that the inquiry will be heard and the desired information is available.

2. Visualize the category of information where answers will be located. To receive information related to my inquiry, use visualization to envision the data stored in the Divine Library and is available.

3. Quiet the mind. Use the same techniques utilized by self-hypnosis, prayer, and meditation. Send out a loving prayer for, or meditate on, receiving guidance from higher dimensions, i.e., spiritual realms.

4. Define exactly what knowledge or insights are desired. Focus intently on receiving a response to the inquiry.

5. Take notes in a notebook of what impressions come to you. As thoughts, feelings, or ideas arrive related to the inquiry, document what comes using words and sketches without judgment.

6. After a time, review notes and interpret. Review the information written down and attempt to interpret the information and determine how it relates to the inquiry.

The above process appears to be very similar to the method I had been using to sketch out the diagrams for my books. I wondered if there were approaches taught by others to receive information by way of the subconscious.

I searched for techniques, processes, or first-hand experiences that might be similar to my process to validate I was on to something even if I could not use traditional science to prove it.

Remote Viewing

I soon came across a field of study known as parapsychology (or psi, as it is known in the field). I was surprised to discover many governments around the world had funded research in the psi field for decades.

The United States government funded similar programs back in the 1970s to study the use of extrasensory perception (ESP), clairvoyance, precognition, and remote viewing among other techniques for the collection of intelligence for government purposes (Kress 1999).

I focused on what is referred to as remote viewing, which involves mentally connecting to a remote target to collect information about the target that is physically inaccessible to a remote viewer. Remote viewing essentially uses a step-by-step, repeatable process for accessing information that is blocked from ordinary perception by time and distance and utilizes something other than the known five senses.

The target's inaccessibility may be due to location, time, or because of shielding of some kind. Some think of remote viewing as the application of extrasensory perception or using one's mind to tune into something unseen.

At first, remote viewing seemed to be unrelated to the process of connecting with the Divine Library. But the more I researched the history of remote viewing and how it had been used over the years, the more I found similarities with what I was working on.

Focused Intention

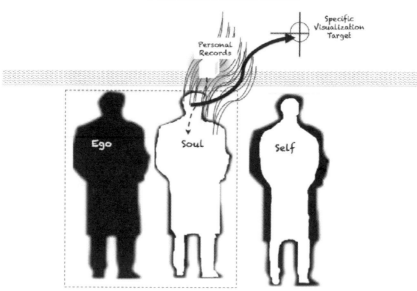

For example, remote viewing uses a very specific protocol (a procedure) to connect and tune into information in an attempt to establish a repeatable systematic process. Remote viewing protocols are intended to minimize mental noise and minimize creative embellishment of a particular target that has been assigned a random identification.

In an interview with Angela Thompson Smith, PhD, an expert in remote viewing and founder of Mindwise Consulting, she said: "There are different methods of remote viewing. The one that Ingo Swann primarily used was a natural psi ability that he called Spontaneous Remote Viewing. This natural method was formalized at Stanford Research Institute (SRI) in order to be researched and studied. It was further developed into the Outbounder, Coordinate, Encrypted Coordinate, and similar protocols. These methods were developed specifically for research purposes. Later, when the United States military became interested, Dr. Hal Puthoff and Ingo Swann formulated a specific protocol called Controlled Remote Viewing (CRV) that uses a strict sequential and formal, written and verbalized, protocol for accessing and recording information from the Matrix. However, the military, prior to the development of CRV, were utilizing a modified version of the SRI Coordinate protocols that they termed Extended Remote Viewing (ERV). ERV utilized a monitor who ensured that the remote viewer remained in an altered state of consciousness, continued to verbalize their perceptions and stayed on task."

Many books, manuals, and technical papers have been written on remote viewing since the early days of research during the 1970s by the Stanford Research Institute and sponsored by the United States government. One such research paper in 1974 concluded: "Our observation of the phenomena leads us to conclude that experiments in the area of so-called paranormal phenomena can be scientifically conducted" (Puthoff et al. 1974).

As I researched numerous techniques and protocols for remote viewing, I found all approaches appeared to use similar techniques to quiet the conscious mind and activate the remote viewer's subconscious to tune into a defined target with the goal of identification or providing information about it.

One such example is described in the paper, "A Suggested Remote Viewing Training Procedure," by G. Scott Hubbard and Gary O. Langford prepared by SRI International in 1986 and sponsored by the US Government. The authors write that the protocol for remote viewing includes the following steps:

▶ Accessing—uniquely identify target, establish need, supply stimulus through a neutral word (target), capture and hold the first impression following the access word.

▶ Objectifying—quickly write down the first impression (correct data will appear vague), take a brief break 10–30 seconds, if any impressions appear vivid and distinct record and circle them. The authors call such impressions "Interpretive Overlays" and write that such impressions are almost always incorrect.

▶ Qualifying—repeat all above steps until target is described in detail. As each impression comes to the viewer, describe target in terms of texture, function, color, age, motion, etc. When description appears complete, end session and receive feedback on the target. (Hubbard and

Langford 1986, 9)

Another more recent example of a remote viewing protocol uses a five-step process described by Dr. Simeon Hein, the director of the Institute for Resonance (instituteforresonance.org/about/) in Boulder, Colorado, as "virtual viewing." The protocol used by Hein includes the steps described as Cool Down, Connecting with the Signal Line, Tuning into the Target's Resonance, Opening the Aperture, Closing the Session (Hein 2010).

I recognized similarities between different remote viewing protocols used by the experts and the organic process I had developed to access the Divine Library. After comparing remote viewing protocols with my organic process of connecting to the Divine Library, I found the steps roughly similar.

I quickly concluded the process I had developed worked reasonably well, providing me with confidence to receive insights about the Divine Library, which I sketched as diagrams for this book.

The biggest main difference with the approach I used and that of remote viewing protocols seemed to be my focused intent and desired objective. In other words, my intent relates to accessing information from the Divine Library to obtain insights and understanding to help me on my spiritual journey, whereas remote viewing is focused on receiving insights and information about a particular target.

It is worth noting that remote viewing experts such as Angela Thompson Smith, PhD, Joseph McMoneagle, and Ingo Swann have also used remote viewing to access off-planet targets such as the rings of Saturn, Mars, the Earth's moon, Jupiter, and many others.

Generally, a typical remote viewing protocol starts by a third party known as a monitor assigned to interface with the remote viewer during the session. A monitor may also be the person who assigns a random number to a specific target. This assignment of a random number is used to keep the remote viewer blind from all information about a particular target. This step prevents the remote viewer from knowing anything more about a target than its random number.

Additionally, there is a double-blind approach used by some protocols to keep both the monitor and the remote viewer unaware of information about a target except for the target's assigned random number.

The use of a random number to represent a target is an important part of the process to eliminate a remote viewer's preconceived notions about a particular target. Once a target has been selected and assigned a random number by the monitor, or another person, the remote viewer focuses on the target by way of the random number cue and performs steps in the remote viewing protocols. Generally, the steps include

▶ **Preparation**

Slow down breathing. Clear the mind. Both the target cue and the desire for information about the target are known to the subconscious and the conscious mind of the remote viewer.

▶ **Tuning**

Activate the subconscious mind. Since the subconscious mind already knows the intent of identifying the target represented by the random number cue, a pencil or pen on a piece of paper is used by the remote viewer to begin sketching. The remote viewer draws by using touch and tracing motions to sketch out whatever impressions come to him or her.

Sketching continues without judgment. The remote viewer allows the process to become automatic while keeping his or her conscious mind quiet. This part of the process is known as creating one or more ideograms or graphic symbols representing the target.

Practitioners believe this step establishes contact with a signal or vibration associated with the target based on the belief that everything has a unique resonance frequency and creates its own energy wave.

Hein suggests the process is similar to that of two tuning forks tuned to the same frequency. When one tuning fork is activated near a second tuning fork, the second tuning fork will automatically begin to vibrate (Hein 2010). For more information about the tuning forks, refer to the reference section of this book for one such example demonstrating the general concept of resonance.

Given impressions received from the subconscious are often very subtle, remote viewers are told it is important to sketch quickly and allow information to flow before the signal breaks off.

▶ **Information Collection**

As information spontaneously flows, the remote viewer becomes aware of feelings and impressions about the target. These are written down with as much detail as possible; the remote viewer sketches whatever comes into his or her mind.

As the remote viewer picks up on sensory information of the target, they are told to write down colors, sounds, contrasts, and other features. The remote viewer opens up to dimensions and magnitudes of the target including its size, shape, pattern, and density.

Finally, the remote viewer opens up to his or her intuitive feelings about the target—how does the target make them feel? The remote viewer notes any surprising feelings or impressions, even if such impressions seem unrelated. Everything is written down.

Throughout this process, the remote viewer is told not to judge or interpret what he or she is writing down.

Another important idea to note as described by remote viewing experts is the belief that the subconscious mind does not talk in words. So information about a target may come in clumps or bursts of images, emotions, and impressions.

▶ **Summary**

Once the target has taken shape on the page, the remote viewer is asked to summarize what he or she has received and describe gut feelings. Practitioners suggest it is important not to judge anything that has been written down.

The remote viewer then sorts out what feels most

accurate and crosses out what does not feel correct. In some remote viewing protocols, crossing-out is discouraged, and all collected data is used for analysis since a remote viewer is not always the best person to judge the received data.

When the summary is complete, the remote viewer is shown the actual target (such as a photograph) and told to look at it. This step provides feedback.

The remote viewer compares the actual target with what was sketched and written down. Practitioners say this step provides feedback to help refine the process and build confidence in the remote viewer.

The last step of verification is intended to allow the remote viewer to calibrate their internal sensing process and tune their subconscious to become more accurate.

There are numerous websites available with remote viewing targets already defined for those inclined to try out the process without a monitor. I highly recommend taking a remote viewing class to learn the various protocols and experience it. I leave it to you to do further research if you have an interest in remote viewing. Interested readers will find reference sources and a few interesting websites in the back of this book. But do your own investigation to discover what resonates with you.

First-Hand Experience

In a remote viewing master class I took from remote viewing expert Angela Thompson Smith, I was taught remote viewing protocols and given numerous targets. My remote viewing experience with one of those targets caused me to have trouble breathing. I found myself overwhelmed with sensory perceptions including disgusting smells, images of wide-open spaces contrasted with cramped spaces, and other interesting perceptions.

When Dr. Smith, acting as my monitor, asked if I was experiencing a physical problem or if the experience felt target related, I told her it was target related and continued with the session.

At the end of the session and before Dr. Smith commented, I made an off-the-cuff remark that she had probably given me a target not located on planet Earth. Later she provided me with feedback on the target. Dr. Smith had given me the target of Pluto.

After the class, I did some further research on Pluto. I discovered from Wikipedia that the atmosphere of Pluto consists mainly of nitrogen, with some methane and carbon monoxide. No wonder I had trouble breathing!

Dr. Smith's class was a fantastic experience for me. I can still smell the full range of disgusting smells from my Pluto target and clearly remember the visuals and feelings from other sessions.

Responses from the Divine Library

Summarizing the process described in an earlier section and personalizing it, my process to access the Divine Library uses the following steps:

1. Trust that the information you are seeking exists.

2. Visualize the category of information where answers are located.

3. Quiet the mind.

4. Define exactly what knowledge or insights are desired.

5. Take notes in a notebook of what impressions come to you.

6. After a time, review notes and interpret.

With a process roughly sketched out to connect to the Divine Library and confidence that other similar techniques such as remote viewing have explored similar questions and techniques for acquiring information, I wondered how exactly a response from the Divine Library arrives in my mind.

I reflected on the past-life regression I had experienced. My experience was like a full- color movie without audio. During the most vivid of my past-life regressions, I experienced a first-person point of view while simultaneously watching it from above. The information during the regression came to me as a burst of thought, which took shape in my brain similar to memories I have from past events.

I confirmed there to be similarities between remote viewing protocols, past-life regression, and my approach to access information from the Divine Library.

I also discovered other processes to access information. For example, in my interview with Dr. Angela Thompson Smith, she pointed out, "There is a protocol called the Christos Experience, specifically developed to mentally travel back in time to experience a past life 'as if' being there physically, emotionally and mentally. It is a powerful technique that allows a subject to be fully immersed in a past life experience."

With respect to regression and hypnotherapy, hypnotherapist Scott Fitzgerald De Tamble pointed out that experiences are different for everyone. "Different people perceive regressions in various sensory modes. Some are visual, some auditory, some kinesthetic, some just intuitive; or combinations of any or all of these. Whether in regressions, remote viewing, meditation, or other ways of mentally/psychically accessing information, the important thing is to be open to whatever impressions you receive" (see Appendix A).

My regression experience was surprising to me. I found the images to be more vivid than reflecting on past memories or remembering a dream. The details of my regression experience stay with me to this day, whereas most of my typical nighttime dreams fade away after a day or two. This first-hand experience gave me a hint of what NDErs mean when they say their NDE was more real than real with vivid colors, e.g., more blue than blue, etc.

While I did not hear any audio with my ears, I did know what was going on. Communication with those during my experience came to me without audio, or telepathically. I heard myself from afar talking to the hypnotherapist who guided me and answered his questions about the scene. But all of the communication within the regression scene I experienced as thought.

Being pragmatic and systematic, I would not have been one that would have embraced such an experience to be possible had I not experienced it first-hand. I suspect the curious reader without such an experience will be a skeptic too. But the cool thing is that I know I experienced what I reported and much more. I honestly feel you can do it too.

My experience was deeply personal. It had a positive impact on me and encouraged me to be more open to the first-hand experiences of others. I believe it was real and not a figment of my imagination.

While part of my experience felt as if I was interacting directly with other souls and Spirit Guides, there was another part of my experience that I would describe as a playback. It would have to be a playback since I was aware of the chair I sat in as I experienced the scene with emotion, images, and communication while under deep hypnosis.

My first-hand experience helped me to validate my approach and understand how a soul's lifetime playback could work.

Given the dynamics of the scenes I experienced, I believe my lifetime moments were collected during an actual prior lifetime experience. Thus, I believe I experienced a partial life playback during my past-life regression.

Could I have imagined the scene or experienced a dream-like scenario? I answer this question no because of the impact the experience had on me. It has stayed with me. There was personal meaning. Comparing the dreams I have experienced all through my life with the vivid experience of past-life regression and between-life hypnotherapy, I concluded there was a distinct difference.

Since it was my first-hand experience, it has become part of my lifetime experience. The experience has become a cherished memory that gives me the confidence to continue asking more profound questions.

Review

For purposes of exploration and discovery, each moment consists of attributes including emotions, syntax, words, thoughts, semantics, events, and other essential elements. Collected moments are grouped into sequences along with the context and ancillary data. A soul's specific lifetime moments are linked with relevant experiences associated with the soul's lifetime experience.

Such linkages make it possible for the soul to replay a life experience while also experiencing how other souls felt during a particular sequence of moments, i.e., events experienced during a lifetime. With the data stored in the Divine Library, it would seem to me that a response must come to me by way of replayed moments as illustrated in the diagram below.

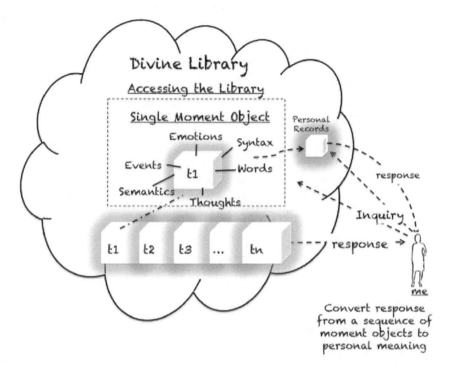

My requests prompt sequences of moments, providing me with the information I have requested. Other responses may be divinely grouped sequences of moments to help me understand a more complicated scenario.

Divinely grouped moments may occur automatically as directed by the soul's inquiry or may involve other souls such as Spirit Guides or souls responsible for Divine Library management to shape soul lifetime moments into meaningful event sequences that provide the requestor with a response and life lesson.

Moment Conversion into Personal Meaning

Continuing with this thought process, it becomes evident that stored moments are more than just pictures stored in an earthly database. Within each moment there are other elements, representing every vibration and energy occurrence within that moment, e.g., emotions such as those illustrated in the moment object figure above.

Conversion and interpretation of moment sequences would seem to be required by the person who made the inquiry and received a response as shown in the figure below.

To further complicate the understanding of responses, there may be many sequences of moments received by the person who made the inquiry, where sequences of moments are all connected, or where other sequences of moments are disjoint.

Building upon these assumptions, the person making the inquiry and receiving the response needs to interpret the moment sequences. Successful interpretation may further imply that the person is ready to receive the response and is open-minded to accurately interpret the information without interference from his or her ego as described in book one.

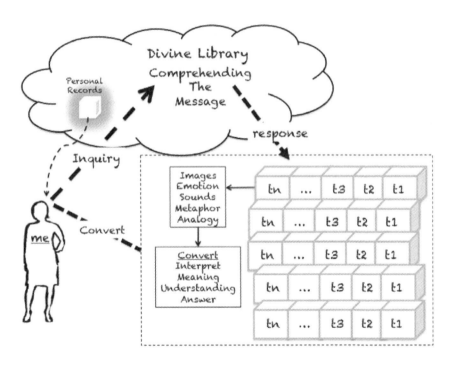

As presented in book one and shown in the figure below, establishing strong connections (items 2 and 6) with the divine storage in higher dimensions (item 1) becomes essential for a person (items 3 and 4) to understand the received response and trust their instincts to interpret the meaning of the response.

It also seems logical to assume that with such a structure and framework, Spirit Guides (item 5) become key contributors to assist the incarnated soul in interpretation and conversion of moment sequences and shaping sequences into meaningful understanding.

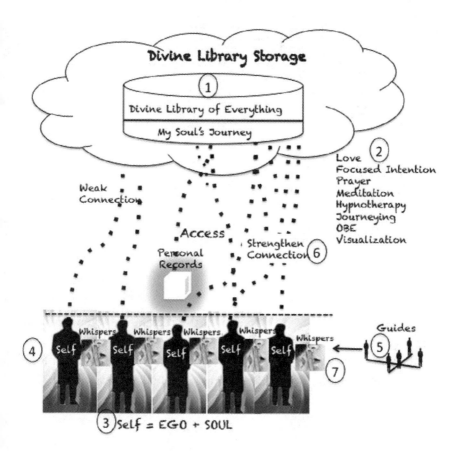

Sequences of events are illustrated below. The self (item 2) makes an inquiry (item 1), which the incarnated soul (item 3) sends to higher dimensions (item 4 and 5). However, the Ego (item 6) can create interference (item 7), preventing the incarnated soul of connecting with the library.

Ultimately, responses return (item 7) to the Self while the soul's guides (item 8) may assist in the process to help the soul convert and understand the responses and shape them into meaningful messages that answer the questions asked.

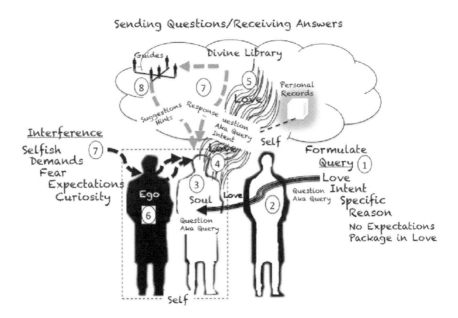

Before I open up my place on the metaphoric elephant with the experiences of others, it is essential to reflect on the Divine Library insights presented in this chapter. The next chapter explores how the Divine Library works for inquiries and responses.

Chapter 4
Insights

Have you ever wondered about a creative insight that came to you out of the blue? Where did the idea originate? How about an ah-ha moment? Have you ever worked on something without any progress until a surprising solution came to you and helped solve what seemed to be an impossible problem? How did that happen?

Most inventors and creative people such as artists, musicians, and authors have experienced ah-ha moments. For a moment or two, we often ask ourselves where the idea or solution came from and how we came up with it, then we passionately get to work on bringing the idea to life.

I used to think that connecting to higher dimensions required a long, difficult journey, a sequence of specific actions, or maybe someone skilled in the art of hypnosis to help me connect with higher dimensions. But with practice and focused intent, I found it possible to travel inward to free my subconscious, enabling me to explore beyond myself. It sounds counterintuitive. Travel inward to explore outward.

By taking the time to reflect and meditate on this concept, I realized we all exist within a cross-section of higher dimensions just like in the story of Flatland where two-dimensional Square lived within Sphere's three-dimensional world. We live our physical lives in the third dimension within many higher dimensions.

We do not think about higher dimensions in that way since our focus and experience is the physical world we see, touch, and feel.

As I extrapolated further, I realized there is no need to travel anywhere to reach higher dimensions since we already exist within them. Apparently, all that is required to journey into higher dimensions is to free our subconscious from our conscious mind. It is our conscious mind that is focused on existence within our three-dimensional world.

It sounds easy. But quieting one's mind is anything but easy in the hustle bustle of daily life. However, silencing one's mind is essential to connect with spiritual realms to access the Divine Library.

Self-Hypnosis: Quieting One's Mind

Quieting one's mind may sound strange and unfamiliar, but it doesn't have to feel that way. All that is required is to visualize what you hope to achieve and work at shutting out everything else. Focus. Send out love and be clear about your intention such as a question you want answered or information you need to know.

Repeat the words of your intention to yourself. Start by focusing on something specific, such as your heartbeat or breathing in and out. The way I do this is by visualizing special moments I have experienced like my regressions. The process often causes me to feel goose bumps. When that occurs, I focus on sustaining and intensifying those goose bumps.

I concentrate on the heaviness of my eyelids while drifting in a dark tunnel toward a distant light. I tell myself I am going deeper to search for answers.

This takes time and practice to perfect. For some people, practicing the same process over and over again becomes a repeatable way to connect to spiritual realms.

Ah-Ha Moments

As I learned while writing book one, some of these ah-ha moments may be related to an original idea that comes from a process happening somewhere deep inside our physical brains. It might be just a random thought prompted by our imagination among hundreds of possible solutions. Or the moment might be a whisper from a Spirit Guide or deceased loved one, providing timely guidance.

Many subjects under hypnosis and NDErs report being told by Spirit Guides to ask for help when one needs it. Apparently, these Spirit Guides want to help us, but they require we assert our free will to ask for help.

Have you ever felt as if you experienced a heavenly nudge, received a sign from a deceased loved one, or felt some heavenly intervention? Most of us have examples, albeit many of us feel uncomfortable talking about our personal experiences.

Our experiences may even feel smaller when we try to explain it in words to someone else. If we stop worrying about the opinions of others and focus on what rings true based on our experiences, we can feel our connection with spiritual realms deepen.

This heavenly connection is deeply personal. You may feel your connection is with God, Spirit Guides, the Source, Spirit, the Universe, or deceased loved ones. What matters most is your personal spiritual connection. It is your perspective. In my opinion, there is no wrong way to approach the connection process as long as the connection is made with love and it feels true to you.

From my perspective, I embrace the notion of Spirit Guides. My belief comes from experience, my research into many hypnotherapy regression sessions, and the past-life regressions I experienced.

Spirit Guides watch over and assist us during our life experience. I embrace this perspective and think of the assistance as spiritual whispers, nudges, or hints. Could Spirit Guides be offering us insights gleaned from the Divine Library?

If Spirit Guides have access to the library, how do they know what information or hints to send us? Does the Divine Library include more than just life experience information about a soul's unique journey?

What about access to the library? Can I access it directly? If I have difficulty quieting my mind, can someone else assist us in accessing the Divine Library?

Refer to the figure below. An incarnated soul or self (item 2) formulates a query (item 1), which is sent (item 4) from the incarnated soul (item 3) to higher dimensions (item 5).

When the inquiry is made, the response (item 7) returns to the incarnated soul (item 3) for interpretation by the self (item 2). As mentioned in the previous chapter, the ego (item 6) can distract the self by making selfish demands, feeling fear, asserting expectations, and making inquiries simply out of curiosity (item 10). Although, I have not found any support for the notion that inquiries made out of curiosity are wrong. I am only suggesting that spending more time on curiosity seeking rather than working on personal growth may be exciting but not personally useful.

However, curiosity or interest may be just the motivator you need to get started on your spiritual journey. You decide what questions to ask and when to ask them. As long as you feel driven to search for a particular answer, I say go for it!

Inquiries that seem to be appropriate in assisting an incarnated soul include the examples (item 12) shown in the figure above. Note that these types of inquiries may have a profound meaning with sincere intent to work through challenges occurring in the incarnated soul's life. Or, as mentioned above, your questions may merely be curiosities.

Note item 13. When I refine my questions with more specificity and clear intent, it seems logical to assume the responses will be more meaningful without requiring extensive translation and personal assumption.

From my experience, responses more often than not come by way of thought information and imagery that the receiver must personally interpret. If one allows a third party to provide the interpretation, it might become a distraction (item 14) or misunderstanding. What truly matters is your understanding. Distractions may also come from uninvited opinions, peer pressure, or self- doubt resulting in misinterpretation of the received responses.

I often must remind myself that we all have our palms outstretched on the metaphoric elephant trying to comprehend and understand higher dimensions in whatever way feels best to us personally.

This may mean developing a personal relationship with spiritual realms in silent meditation as discussed above, sharing ideas with like-minded groups, or using a teacher (item 10) to assist with one's spiritual journey. It also means that there are most likely different answers to the questions we ask, depending on perspective and intent.

I am a curious soul on a spiritual journey, so it is important to me to experience the journey through personal experience. I remain open to other ideas, support, insights, perspectives, and alternative ways of thinking from others sharing this moment around me.

That said, I empower myself to take ownership of my lifetime, my spiritual journey, and my personal experience. No matter what others say or assert, I am the one in charge of my physical lifetime. As such, I must connect with spiritual realms in my unique way just as I recommend you do too.

Practical Application of the Records

As I explored the Divine Library, it became logical to extrapolate and seek answers about other types of records that might be stored in the library to test my assertion that moment records are essential to record everything that is possible to record to facilitate the soul's learning process.

The figure below shows a rough sketch of how I visualize the storage of soul records or soul books in the Divine Library and the process for accessing them.

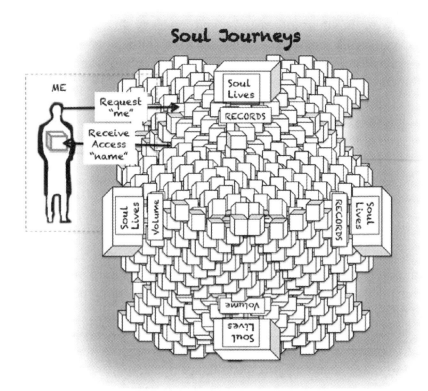

Moment objects are stored as collections of soul lifetime experiences, comprising one volume or category of data in the Divine Library. Additionally, the Divine Library is jam-packed with an infinite number of volumes and categories with each containing an endless amount of moment objects from the beginning of physical existence from an infinite number of points of view.

Further, each volume in the library must contain information such as incarnation options, different soul schools, and specific soul journeys. In addition, I envision there to be data links pointing to raw data where each link represents one or more points of view or other data.

Using a data link to reference raw data avoids the need to duplicate the raw data storage for each and every soul's book.

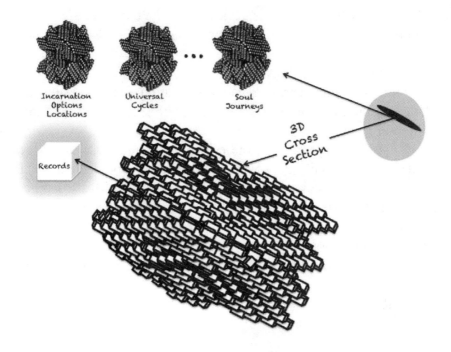

For example, if I embrace what physicists call the multiverse, I know that the theory postulates the existence of many different universes beyond the universe we live in. I like to think of it as bubbles in a bathtub. Inside of each bubble exists a universe, and we all exist within one of those bubbles.

Taking the idea of a multiverse and extrapolating a bit more, apply the same logic on a universe level that is implemented on a soul level where all moments are being recorded and stored to facilitate soul learning. This further assumes each universe has its own set of moment objects since the first moment that universe came into existence (e.g., Big Bang).

With this idea in mind, I continue to extrapolate and imagine cycles naturally occurring in every universe such as the life-death cycle of each biological creature and the life-death cycle of stars and planets.

Next, I apply the basic concept that souls are incarnated on the Earth school to learn while environmental cycles are at play related to the physical world (Earth). This concept supports the idea that Earth is only one such school in the universe, multiverse, and other dimensions as Cannon and others believe (Cannon 2011, 9–10).

In fact, if one thinks deeper about cycles on Earth and in our universe, we know astronomers tell us that our sun will eventually fade and the cycle of our solar system will begin a new cycle in a different form.

I must reiterate that these ideas about universe life cycles and solar systems like our solar system are not put out there to create fear. In fact, the ideas are just a logical extension of what astronomers have already established. I am simply enhancing the concept with the learning journey of a soul in an attempt to comprehend the data types that are stored in other volumes within the Divine Library.

During the interview memorialized in Appendix A with hypnotherapist Scott Fitzgerald De Tamble, I ask Scott about the insights reported by his clients while under deep hypnosis. Here is a sample of that interview:

Richard: *Have you come across any discussion of information in the library that is not soul-specific? That is, of a more general nature?*

Scott: Yes. Some clients have indicated that the library contains information on the general history of Earth, other planets, star systems, and galaxies that souls may have incarnated within; and cosmological information about the creation and history of the entire universe.

I've had a few clients access technical knowledge in their chosen fields of science, engineering, physics, medicine, and other areas of study.

There is also information on ethics, philosophy, systems of thought, emotion, behavior, and so many things. As far as I can tell, the library is pretty much a cornucopia of knowledge and records, a sort of super-Wikipedia of Everything.

The library seems to hold information on everything that has ever existed or occurred on every dimension, including thoughts, feelings, dreams, animal, vegetable, mineral, Devic kingdoms, spiritual, angelic, perhaps even motions of atoms . . . it's all recorded. You might say the library is "God's Memory." (Appendix A)

Why am I so interested in the other moments beyond a soul's data stored in the library? What if we could seek other data such as data related to experiences and lessons learned by ancient civilizations on Earth as well as other civilizations on other worlds in the universe? Or lessons learned from other universes within the multiverse or other dimensions?

What if we could collectively change our present life experience on Earth for the better by receiving insights from experiences beyond our Earth school? What if we could use this knowledge to reduce the amount of suffering required to learn lessons in the Earth school by working together to shape our physical world with wisdom stored in the Divine Library?

After understanding my desire to access the records stored in the Divine Library, I wonder how to get my head around the notion that I can request other volumes of moments stored in the Divine Library.

The idea is a bit daunting. It would be like entering a library as extensive as a country with the goal of finding a single book in some house located somewhere in the country. But even that example does not convey the magnitude of data stored in the Divine Library.

Perhaps a better visualization might be thinking of the Divine Library as if each volume in the library was a single grain of sand. Wherein the Divine Library contains all the grains of sand on every world in the universe.

As I work with the Divine Library more amazing insights come to me. It feels as if the entire Divine Library is a conscious, living entity that is an ever-evolving, ever-moving, self-entwined energy system, continually making new connections, pathways, and records.

So how do I access a specific volume within the Divine Library? How do I ask for permission to access the Divine Library to view moment sequences? Who do I ask?

If I further assume energy beings or other divine beings are responsible for managing the content stored in the Divine Library, I need to learn how to communicate with the heavenly beings to request library access.

Given my personal past-life regression experience, I am confident there is structure everywhere even in higher dimensions. But how can I send meaningful inquiries to the Divine Library?

After much thought, a lightbulb went on inside my head. Why not just ask the right question and let my Spirit Guides interface with other responsible entities to help me find the information I am seeking?

I realized I don't need to access the information directly. I just need to trust my guides to assist me. My questions would merely need to be concise, clear, and with loving intention. All I need to do is send the request for information.

If my request is beyond my need to know or if the timing is not right to receive the information, my guides will simply prepare me to receive the information or refocus me on other learning experiences until the timing is right.

I concluded that all I need to do is ask the right question with loving intent, knowing in my heart that the Divine Library consists of moment recordings. The stored data is organized such that a soul can efficiently learn from it. The more a soul learns about the information stored in the Divine Library, it seems the more the soul can access it.

The following diagram shows examples of the types and categories of information and data linkages that may be stored in the Divine Library. It also shows other spiritual entities represented by the label librarians who assist with the record-accessing process:

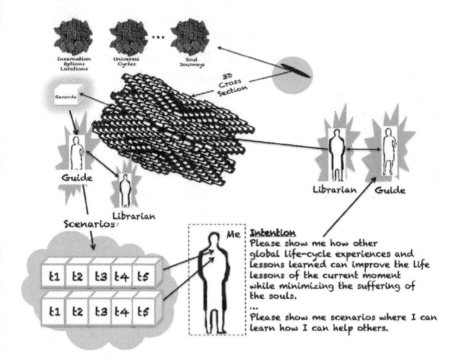

Question Examples

Why don't beings in higher dimensions fix the problems on Earth for us? Solve our environmental, social, and political issues? Why don't these beings minimize the suffering we experience during a lifetime?

Do these questions sound familiar?

I asked many of these questions in book one. I concluded that beings in higher dimensions are not able (for whatever reason—actual or rule-based) to fix our three-dimensional realm. That said, it does seem as if there are always exceptions to rules when it comes to comprehending higher dimensions.

Maybe it is up to incarnated souls to collectively evolve the physical space with which we embody. I tend to embrace this way of thinking for many reasons, but the most important reason relates to the lessons souls are learning.

Sure, there are individual lessons as described, but apparently, there are also collective lessons that are being learned by groups of souls. As such, it becomes our incarnated responsibility to fix our messes, which includes the physical environment.

We incarnated souls who are living in this particular moment in time are responsible for reconfiguring our earthly laws and regulations to be more in line with love and growth. It is up to us to address the needs of all incarnated souls at this moment in linear time.

As I continue to contemplate the notion of collective lessons and the idea that only incarnated souls can shape the world in which we inhabit through action and circumstance, I can look to the Divine Library as a resource with which to gain insights, knowledge, and guidance. It is up to each one of us to tend to our physical world and collectively shape it into the place we want it to be.

More Questions

To receive the information needed to solve earthly problems, I must craft new questions that can be asked in order to receive meaningful insights and responses.

o "Please show me how other global life-cycle experiences and lessons learned from beyond Earth can improve the life lessons of the current moment to minimize the suffering of the souls presently incarnated on this Earth school."

o "Please show me scenarios where I can learn how I can help other souls move past [a problem] that is not allowing them to progress."

o "Please show those souls who are ready to receive the information to open their hearts up to find solutions to rebalance our Earth school and repair the damage we have made over many lifetimes."

You get the idea.

Since I believe the information must exist, all I need to do is send out a request with loving intention to make incarnated life on Earth the most loving and efficient life experience possible for incarnated souls. Optimizing our Earth school would not only make soul lessons more rewarding, but it would also help our experiences become more joyful and less painful.

While I can send love out into the world to try and raise the vibration of other incarnated souls, it does no good if other incarnated souls are not receptive. A more effective way to accomplish the objective of assisting incarnated souls might be to ask for help from our Spirit Guides to be our Divine Library advocates.

I can ask my Spirit Guide by using a little prayer to search the Divine Library for solutions and suggestions that best fit the circumstance—describe a concern in detail with the loving desire to find answers to solve problems. You may decide to meditate or find a quiet spot where you can reflect and ask for help.

For some readers who have never tried such a thing, this may feel strange, awkward, or even embarrassing. If that describes you, choose a place and time of day where you can find a private location to calm yourself, meditate, then send off your prayer.

From my experience, answers will come, but most often the answers I have received are very subtle. If I am not paying attention, I might even miss a response.

If you start to feel frustrated because you think your efforts are not effective, just trust that answers will come when the time is right.

For me, some answers arrive when my mind is on something else entirely. Sometimes it takes a long time. Other times answers arrive quickly. But in all cases, responses were not an external force fixing something for me nor did answers arrive by way of words being whispered in my ear.

In my experience, once answers arrive, the information feels like subtle suggestions, insights, and ideas. Each one of us must ultimately choose to act on our intuition or not. I try to remember this simple guideline: when my intention to receive answers is sent out with love, and the received suggestion, insight, or idea feels in my gut as if it has been sent to me from higher dimensions with love, then the message is from the Divine Library.

I end this chapter with loving intention that the message of using Spirit Guides to facilitate study in the Divine Library resonates with incarnated souls who are ready to receive information and try the approach.

If lots of us ask our Spirit Guides to reveal timeless lessons to help us solve our present challenges, I am hopeful we can collectively shape our lives and this Earth school into a more joyful learning environment, allowing us to learn our desired lessons.

Chapter 5
Perspectives

With a frame of reference established for the Divine Library, this chapter researches additional perspectives concerning accessing, interpreting, and understanding information in the Divine Library. These perspectives include the application of a sacred prayer, insights from subjects under deep hypnosis, and channeling.

Sacred Prayers

In their books, Ernesto Ortiz, Jiyuh Chyan, and Linda Howe discuss the use of prayer to access the Akashic Records or what I refer to as the Divine Library in this book.

Ortiz uses what he refers to as a sacred Mayan prayer and says the process is more than simply reading a prayer, "We must prepare carefully and keep an open heart to connect with the Records and receive the information" (Ortiz 2015, 26).

Howe refers to the practice of accessing the Akashic Records using prayer as part of the connection process, which she describes as "part of the sacred prayer process of accessing the Records" (Howe 2010, 11–12).

Chyan offers a universal prayer to access the Akashic Records. She says of the different prayers available to access the Records, "It totally depends on which one resonates with you most" (Chyan 2017, 21).

As mentioned in the last chapter, my approach to prayer is to focus my intention and open my heart. I have come to realize I do not use a specific prayer. Rather, my prayer simply begins with an offering of thanks for all I have learned in my life and a short preamble, describing why I am in need of assistance. Then I focus on the specific information of my request. I try to describe as clearly as possible why receiving a response to my inquiry is important to me.

Finally, I state my request with gratitude and love. Most of the time I do not wait for an answer. Rather, I ask for the answer to come to me when the time is right.

Deep State of Hypnosis

In their books referenced below, Dr. Michael Newton and Dolores Cannon share information about a spiritual library gleaned from many hypnotherapy sessions with their subjects. Scott Fitzgerald De Tamble also discusses this subject with me in an interview documented in Appendix A.

Memorialized in his books, Dr. Michael Newton documents experiences of his subjects under deep hypnosis who often reference a spiritual library and describe accessing an individual book with their name inscribed on it. I have also found in my research that some people recognize their name when they open the book inscribed on the first page in many different languages.

Each individual book is said to represent a specific soul's journey over many lifetimes. In his book Destiny of Souls: New Case Studies of Life Between Lives, Newton says about the spiritual library and "Life Books" described by his subjects, "Everyone tells me the location of the Life Books is seen as a huge study hall, in a rectangular structure, with books lined along walls and many souls studying at desks who do not seem to know each other" (Newton 2000, 150).

Hypnotherapist and author Dolores Cannon discusses her experiences and the insights that have come from client sessions within her books. She writes, "Many, many of my clients have described this Library the same way. It is where all knowledge is kept, everything that is known and will ever be known. It also has the Akashic Records, which are the records of every life that has ever been lived since the creation" (Cannon 2011, 11).

In her book, Between Life and Death, Cannon says, "This library in the spirit realm was not a strange place for me. I have journeyed there many times with the aid of my subjects. Several have mentioned it and their descriptions vary only slightly." Cannon goes on to say of her subjects in a deep state of hypnosis, "Other people are in groups or walking round silently carrying manuscripts and books to different places . . . They're studying. Everybody has a sense of purpose, and there's serenity" (Cannon 1993, 90).

In my interview with Scott Fitzgerald De Tamble, C Ht, in Appendix A, he discusses the library as reported by his clients under deep hypnosis. He refers to them as Life Between Lives® (LBL) hypnotherapy:

> LBL sessions are rather lengthy, often running three to four hours or more. As mentioned, clients may have many and diverse experiences within a session; but a visit to the library can often bring that special insight that opens new avenues and opportunities. Because of the existence and accessibility of their own soul histories, people are able to gain a higher perspective of the goals, purposes, activities, relationships, and challenges in the current lifetime.
>
> With this longer view, we can often spot recurring themes and patterns throughout their lifetimes, and thus more clearly understand the portent of whatever dramas may be transpiring in the here and now. In reading about, viewing, or immersing into a previous lifetime's records, clients are able not only to review their own experiences, but are also able to understand the impact they may have had on other people, and on subsequent events.
>
> Knowledge acquired in our visits to the library often inspires a person to make more beneficial choices and actions in their current life. There is much more to the library, but this is how we tend to utilize it in our LBL sessions. (Appendix A)

Channeling—Edgar Cayce

Another interesting source of first-hand experience is from a man named Edgar Cayce (1877–1945), whom biographer Jess Stearn referred to as the "Sleeping Prophet" (Stearn 1967).

During his life, Edgar Cayce gave thousands of readings for people while he was in a trance state. Many of these readings involved medical diagnosis, past-life readings, and future prophecies.

Cayce founded a nonprofit in 1931 known as the Association for Research and Enlightenment (ARE) to research and explore holistic health, personal spirituality, intuition, reincarnation, philosophy, dreams, and ancient mysteries. Cayce put himself into a trance to channel insights for subjects from the Book of Life, God's Book of Remembrance, or Akashic Records.

In Edgar Cayce on the Akashic Records, Kevin J. Todeschi writes about Cayce's readings. Todeschi references Cayce's Case 294-19 Report File, which described Cayce's process of doing readings for an individual, involving apparently entering a trance state then leaving his physical body. Presumably, this implied Cayce would have an out-of-body experience where Cayce's consciousness would travel to spiritual realms. Additionally, Todeschi cites Cayce's reading 1650-1 regarding information to which Cayce gained access, including the thoughts, deeds, and activities of the individual (Todeschi 1998).

Finding One's Place on the Metaphoric Elephant

Many readers continue to ask me, "Why are there so many perspectives about spirituality? Which one is correct?"

I remind them that I believe each perspective comes from a different location on the metaphoric spiritual elephant described in book one. This is because each of us has a unique perspective based on life experience, upbringing, beliefs, and education. While we may share fundamental aspects of the bigger picture perspective, the finer details remain very personal.

An approach I use to sort out the many different perspectives is to focus on what resonates with me. It does not mean that views that do not resonate are wrong. I am suggesting that each of us must connect with higher dimensions from an individual perspective and discover what is personally meaningful and what is not. We must find our own truth.

Spiritual journeys are a personal experience. Do what feels right to you. As for my spiritual journey as an inventor and creative person, I have always enjoyed doing research, experiments, and independent study to search for answers.

I choose not to debate or promote one perspective, technique, or approach to spirituality over any other since all the references incorporated in my books come from first-hand experiences. Instead, I embrace all perspectives without feeling any particular perspective threatens my way of thinking. In my opinion, it is worth the time to study first-hand experiences and the beliefs of others. There is much to be learned.

Similarities and Differences

What can we learn by so many different approaches for accessing the Divine Library? One observation consistent with my original thought process is to enter into a mind-calming state such as trance, meditation, prayer, or hypnosis.

In the book The Isaiah Effect, Gregg Braden writes of the feelings a prayer's words evoke, "The power of prayer is found in a force that cannot be spoken or transmitted as the written word" (Braden 2000, 146).

It appears that once our conscious mind has been silenced and our subconscious takes over, only then can we access higher dimensions and information within the Divine Library. To access information, one must be specific, projecting loving intentions and focusing on a detailed question.

In all approaches, the art of formulating specific questions is essential. However, interpretation of responses can be confusing no matter the approach.

I found it fascinating that Newton, Cannon, De Tamble, and many others have used deep hypnosis for years to access between-life memories from their subjects. While approaches are different, the process resulted in similar outcomes with subjects who talked about a spiritual library and soul life books. These hypnotherapy approaches reveal a spiritual library independent from others such as Cayce using trance, or Howe, Chyan, and Ortiz, who recite different prayers and refer to the library as the Akashic Records.

This referenced first-hand experience from numerous sources reporting similar descriptions of a Divine Library gives me confidence about my efforts to comprehend the Divine Library. Thus, my earlier deductions are for the most part in line with insights from Akashic Records teachers, spiritual channels, and hypnotherapy experts.

While Ortiz, Chyan, and Howe's approaches use different prayers, their techniques are similar in that they start off with a loving prayer to initiate the process to connect with the Akashic Records, provide focus, and establish intention.

After learning of their approaches, I realized that I too had started off with a personalized prayer to initiate my search for answers about the Divine Library for this book. As previously described, my approach has been more freestyle and personal to me, involving writing and sketching versus reciting a specific prayer to open records or putting myself in a trance. My approach for accessing the Divine Library has evolved into a combination of informal prayer, channeling, and remote viewing.

For this book, my simple prayer asks for guidance, helpful information to share with the world, and insights that inspire confidence to ask big questions. But I encourage you to use an approach that personally resonates with you to access the Divine Library.

It appears to be a shared opinion among teachers and practitioners that helpful spirits or spiritual librarian entities are involved in Divine Library management on some level.

Differences between these viewpoints include details such as how heavenly entities manage the library and access control. My approach to access the Divine Library is to keep it simple by asking for assistance in retrieving information. I do this through a free-style prayer, meditation, or by focused intent.

Timing

One of the many lessons I have learned on this journey is that timing is an essential part of the entire process. When timing is aligned with Spirit Guide assistance, have confidence that the responses you seek will come.

I believe using Spirit Guides to access the Divine Library to answer questions has built-in constraints. For example, if it is not time for me to know my life purpose or which decision to make for whatever reason, I will not receive information or response until it is the right time. It is as simple as that. Additionally, sometimes an answer comes that we feel is the wrong answer but in time we come to realize that it was the right answer.

This approach is consistent with many of the near-death experiences discussed in book one. During an NDE, some NDErs report being told they must return to their physical life because it is not their time to return home in the spiritual realms, i.e., the person still has work to do in their present life. Upon returning to their life, the NDEr remembers talking about purpose with spiritual entities, but cannot remember what he or she had been told about their life purpose.

I know if I were told I still had more to do in my life, I would attempt to ask a long list of new questions starting with the word why. Maybe the reason NDErs do not remember is simply related to timing.

As I reflect and focus on the idea that timing is essential, it is clear that knowing everything about one's life purpose without having experienced or gone through an important learning process would be like cheating on a math test.

Sure you might get an A+ on the math test, but you'd walk out of that classroom not fully understanding how to work through the math problems. You would also leave without a sense of accomplishment and confidence that you can succeed at challenging tasks.

For me, if I ask questions and it becomes clear that I am not making progress in my search for answers, I assume it is not time to know the answer. I move on.

Dwelling on such things would most likely become a huge distraction and might even prevent me from experiencing the present moments that must be experienced to prepare me to learn my purpose.

That said, it seems to me there are some questions where knowing enough to ask the right question is all that is needed—sort of implied timing. Think about that idea.

If I lived before the time of the steam engine, I would not

know what questions to ask about steam engines, unless, of course, I am an inventor who dreams up the idea to build the machine that uses steam to automate human activities.

Or maybe I tapped into the Divine Library and knew enough about steam and mechanical devices to receive such ideas. Only then might I become one of the inventors of the steam engine.

After the steam engine is built, many more people would see it in action and know enough to ask more questions about how a steam-powered engine works. For example, how can heating up water move a heavy mechanism? That idea sounds impossible. How could water power an engine? It sounds crazy. When the details are worked out and we see a steam engine in action, steam engines become obvious.

In my opinion, those who do not believe such a divine resource exists or those who cannot imagine how such a spiritual information system might work will not understand enough to access it.

When I compare notes from other perspectives sharing the opinion that a Divine Library exists, I am motivated to ask deeper questions and learn how to access the Divine Library effectively.

Chapter 6
Future

I began an exploration of time in book one by suggesting that time in the fourth dimension (four spatial dimensions) would likely act differently than time in our physical world of three dimensions where time consists of past, present, and future. Our time can be thought of as a single line segment of moments, or a timeline, with everything occurring in each moment on the timeline.

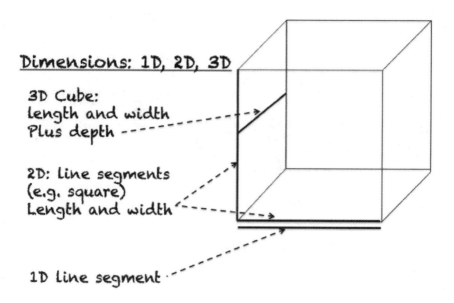

Dimensions: 1D, 2D, 3D

3D Cube:
length and width
Plus depth

2D: line segments
(e.g. square)
Length and width

1D line segment

Driven by the experiences of NDErs, OBErs, and those who have experienced regressions, I postulated that within four spatial dimensions time might transform from a single line segment to something much more complex.

Perhaps time in the fourth dimension incorporates an additional dimension of to-and-fro, where an infinite number of line segments are all wrapped together. A single timeline segment could then be isolated and selected for a particular incarnation. In other words, during the incarnation planning stage, a soul (or group of souls) would pick out a desired timeline to associate with an incarnation.

A to-and-fro dimension might be like a ball of threads, as shown in the figure below, where each line segment timeline is a single thread with a unique past, present, and future.

Each thread of time is causality-based, representing one of an infinite number of lifetime scenarios in the third dimension where each timeline is dependent upon key decisions made by all incarnated souls sharing the timeline.

A Higher Dimension Version of Time

An infinite number of linear timelines, each with a unique past, present, future timeline.

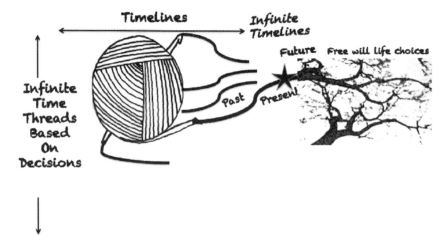

For example, the "to" part of to-and-fro may allow a soul to view possible linear timelines based on probabilities and critical life events. For the "fro" part of to-and-fro, the soul might view lifetime events and possible decisions made by the soul and the possible effects of those decisions during a lifetime.

For those readers wondering how all time can exist in a single moment as many experiencers have reported, just imagine this ball of timeline threads from the fourth dimension. It seems possible for all time to exist like that of the ball of yarn analogy. This is an example of why perspective matters. Regardless of how time is configured in higher dimensions, viewing time from those higher dimensions provides a different perspective than viewing time from our three-dimensional universe.

All I did to observe time from a different perspective was apply a thought experiment—if one dimension of time exists, two dimensions of time must exist, and so on. Next, I incorporated information gleaned from countless experiencers into what seemed reasonable to support their reported experiences. I also know from first-hand experience in this three-dimensional physical universe that time consists of a timeline of moments comprising everything that occurs, moment by moment, on the timeline. I apply the proposed concepts, extrapolate, and attempt to visualize this model of time working in higher dimensions.

In the fourth dimension, souls might have easy access to move between an infinite number of past, present, and future times on an infinite number of line segment timelines.

Perhaps in future books, I will explore this idea in more detail as it applies to a soul's third-dimension life planning and life experience. For now, this explanation is used to merely demonstrate that during life planning, between-life soul study sessions, and life reviews, replaying life experiences could be accomplished by accessing a single thread of time and replaying all the applicable moments stored on that timeline.

This imagined perspective of time in higher dimensions would presumably allow a soul to move between time threads to facilitate the soul's education and learning experience. This perspective is consistent with NDE life reviews, where a soul learns by replaying key lifetime events, replaying decisions made, and experiencing probable effects of life choices.

Reflecting on the soul's incarnated lifetime by replaying different timeline threads to comprehend free will decisions would be an amazing approach to learning from physical life experiences.

The process would also enable a soul to reflect on the impact of decisions during a lifetime experience.

Given that the system and the Divine Library aid a soul in learning, it is logical to assume the same method can be applied using a slightly different configuration to assist the soul and the soul's Spirit Guides with planning and modeling a soul's future lifetime as illustrated below.

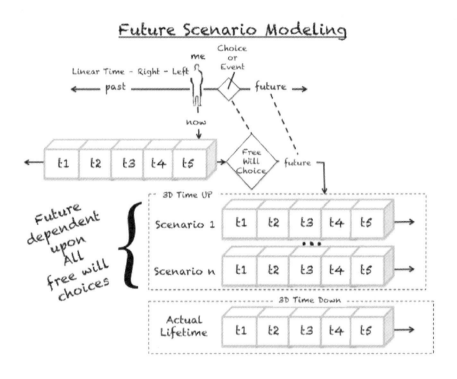

The moments stored in the Divine Library would include all of the above information associated with a soul's collection of lifetime experiences. Each soul book would consist of all information related to the planning of each lifetime and every moment that occurred during the actual lifetime. Every experienced lifetime would also include summary data reflecting decisions made when each significant event occurred during the soul's experienced incarnated lifetime.

The next question most of us ask is this one: does that mean every possible cause-effect sequence and decision selected is known during a lifetime? I would say no from the perspective of a soul because there would be nothing for the soul to learn nor would there be anything to study after a lifetime. In my opinion, incarnated souls would be puppets. From all that I have learned, I do not believe that is the case at all.

In many of the sessions reported by experienced professionals including Newton, Cannon, De Tamble, and my insights, soul training, modeling, and other activities occur in between physical lifetime as illustrated in the figure below.

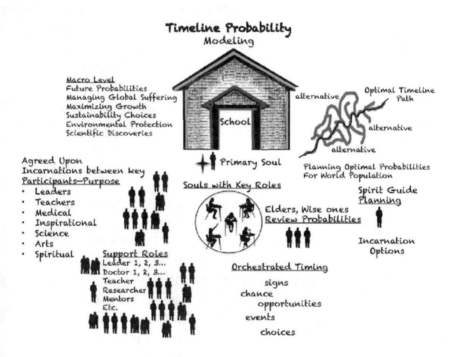

Practitioners including Cannon, De Tamble, and Newton have reported their subjects under deep hypnosis speak of soul life planning and training between incarnations.

Such planning includes

o Selection of support souls and soul mates with whom
  to incarnate
o Selection of a life process, purpose, focus
o Objectives to be explored during the lifetime
o Lessons the soul wants to learn
o Layout of key events that will occur during the lifetime
o Other important lifetime elements and features.

The figure below illustrates a particular moment in linear time during a soul's incarnation. The moment represents all of the souls and relationships associated with a particular soul's life experience. To assist in differentiating one soul from another, the relationships are illustrated from the point of view of one soul defined as the primary soul.

Item 1 represents close family and friend relationships with support souls from the perspective of the primary soul labeled as "me."

Item 2 represents the overlapping relationships from the perspective of the primary soul's wife.

Item 3 represents overlapping relationships from the perspective of the primary soul's workmate.

Item 4 represents overlapping relationships from the perspective of a primary soul's "close friend."

Note that the moment in time t1 reflected in the figure below occurs simultaneously for each of the interacting souls, resulting in overlapping relationships. This illustration highlights how relationships change over time and how interactions between souls are essential to a primary soul's incarnated lifetime experience.

The illustration also reinforces the importance of life planning and the various roles that individual souls play within the lifetime experience of another soul.

The figure shows the complexity of mapping out billions of primary souls existing together in a single moment of time and interacting over many moments of time. I believe the perspective further reinforces the notion that we are all genuinely connected with every soul who shares moment "t1" with us.

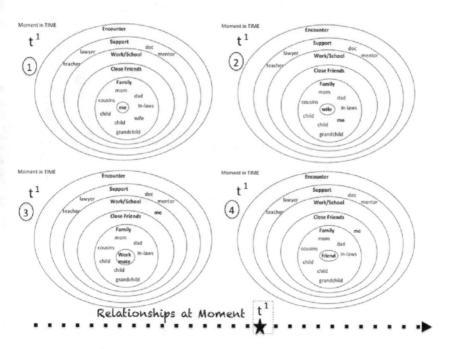

Soul life planning and training further consists of sketching out cause-effect scenarios. This includes defined events that are intended to occur at key moments in time during a primary soul's incarnated lifetime.

I think of this process as a soul life graph illustrated in the figure below. It includes major lifetime events shown by the circles, major life choices shown by the decision diamonds, and smaller life choices in darkened diamonds resulting in a minor path change.

The graph incorporates both the soul's decisions and external events that have an impact on the primary soul due to the soul's assertion of free will and the free will assertion by other souls.

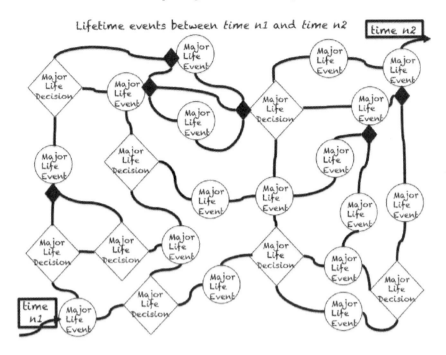

Lifetime events between time n1 and time n2

During the primary incarnated soul's lifetime, there are interactions with many other incarnated souls. Some interactions are preplanned, while some interactions occur due to cause- effect scenarios. Still, other interactions result from a combination of the soul's free will and free will asserted by other souls with whom moments are shared.

The illustration below represents an example of a primary soul's incarnated lifetime encounters on a shared timeline (8) with other souls (9).

It provides an example of how a primary incarnated soul (1) labeled "me" might move through a lifetime (7) experience in linear time while interacting with other incarnated souls (2, 3, 4, 5, 6).

The primary incarnated soul's (1) line intersects with the lines of other incarnated souls.

This interaction represents intersections during a lifetime, where each incarnated soul in the illustration additionally experiences their incarnated lifetime (2) from their perspective as a primary incarnated soul.

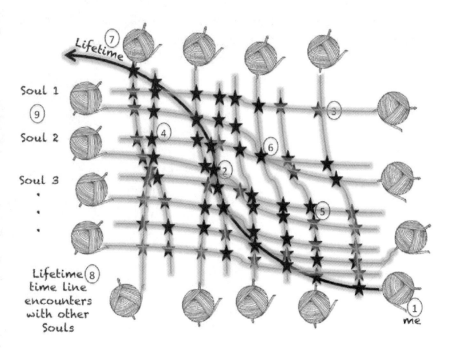

I would have never imagined how each one of our lifetime journeys could be so profoundly personal yet so beautifully interwoven. Viewing one soul's lifetime journey mapped with hundreds of other incarnated soul journeys, intersecting at different moments during a lifetime, is nothing short of miraculous.

These illustrations show how we can all be connected and experiencing this lifetime together. The more we recognize the value of helping each other, the more we are able to understand how to help ourselves.

Visualizing the nature of significant life events and decisions occurring during a lifetime illustrates the importance and impact of free will, cause, and effect during an incarnated soul's lifetime experience.

Focusing on accessing the Divine Library to provide insights to enhance the journey of all souls feels like a good reason to continue asking more questions and querying the Divine Library.

The insights explored in this chapter suggested data exists beyond a specific soul's journey. In the next chapter, the Divine Library will be accessed to discover more general insights. I will keep each new inquiry wrapped in a prayer of hope and focused with pure intention to do my best to present meaningful insights and cultivate ideas that may help us on our spiritual journey.

Chapter 7
Events, Patterns, and Scenario Linkages

I am amazed how each of our personal spiritual journeys and lifetime learning experiences are incredibly unique and miraculous. The between-life soul experiences documented in books by Cannon, Newton, and others suggest that souls can study specific topics of interest between incarnations.

Given the idea that everything is recorded during a soul's incarnated lifetime, there must be an infinite number of emotional subcategories to organize moment sequences for learning purposes such as kindness, selfishness, happiness, loss, love, successes, anger, etc.

Such categories provide a plurality of experiences arranged by learning topics that can be isolated and studied by a soul. Without an ability to analyze short life experience events of topic- specific moment segments, an entire soul's lifetime would need to be examined. Such a procedure would be extremely inefficient if a soul wanted to simply study one particular emotional experience.

Starting from a single soul and working outward, it seems to me that the most efficient way to manage recorded moments is to link the moment sequences by topics of interest. Using linkages to many soul lifetime experiences eliminates the need to duplicate massive amounts of raw soul lifetime data. The linkages essentially connect to particular recorded events within a soul's lifetime facilitating study of specific areas of interest.

Another volume or category of data comprises a group of incarnated soul lifetimes experienced together. Numerous sources including Cannon, Newton, and others share the regression experiences from subjects who speak of a group of souls incarnating together into a familiar physical environment, or soul school, such as Earth.

With many worlds, universes, and dimensions available to incarnate, experience, and learn, the types of learning experiences are apparently infinite. Given the complexities of countless soul interactions, an excellent way to visualize how the incarnation of a group of souls might work is to start from a single soul and move outward as illustrated in the previous chapter. From a soul's point of view, one group of souls may consist of immediate family, close friends, extended family, friends, workmates, etc.

When moment objects related to the soul are stored, cross-reference information linkages can be created to map out important relationships between the soul and other souls. Life experience data would be collected and stored from all related souls such that the soul is able to experience life events from multiple points of view during a life review process by way of linkages to the lifetime moments of other interacting souls.

The linkages of all stored life experience moments may take the form of a soul group book associated with a group of souls where all soul relationships and lifetime experiences are linked together.

Why is this idea of categories and linkages worth exploring? One reason is to answer the question many have asked regarding how it is possible for NDErs to experience a life review playback from the point of view of all related souls interacting with a particular soul.

With linkages established as suggested, it becomes feasible that such a variable point of view life review playback is logically possible. Extending the concept of linkages, other linkage volumes may exist as illustrated below, including events, places, and scenarios. These linkages would be available to all souls as learning tools.

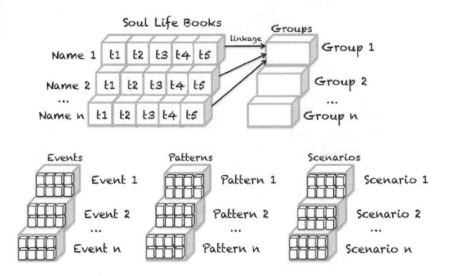

Key lifetime events from a particular soul's book may then be linked to different books such as event, patterns, and scenario soul books.

Given the power of free will and its importance for a soul's life experience, planned lifetime events may or may not happen. Major events agreed upon during pre-incarnation planning can also be described as life markers, wherein there may exist many life markers comprising life scenarios a soul wants to experience where each one is linked to one or more events. There may also be planned situations that are not encountered due to the assertion of free will and cause-and-effect scenarios.

It is worth noting that the idea of preplanning and predefined events or markers is not to say the soul's entire incarnated lifetime is preplanned. Based on reports from hypnotherapy regression sessions, I think of this planning process between lifetimes as sort of a rough sketch or life outline identifying roles, general scenarios, and possible events desired during the soul's next lifetime.

General Linkages

Other linkages within the Divine Library worth noting include moment information associated with specific scenarios reflecting soul patterns of behavior repeated by the soul over many lifetime experiences.

► Some patterns may reflect loving intention.

► Some patterns may not reflect loving intention or action.

Identifying patterns of behavior and linking them with scenarios makes it quite efficient for a soul to learn from a previous life experience while replaying scenes reflecting patterns of behavior. Given the number of moments recorded during a lifetime is presumably incredibly large, it makes sense there would be a methodology to quickly reference scenarios related to patterns of soul behavior.

In other words, scenarios of the soul's lifetime moments associated with patterns of kindness, selfishness, love, anger, charity, etc. As mentioned, linkages to a soul group enables the soul to replay scenarios from the point of view of other family members, close friends, or other incarnated souls in the group.

It is interesting that the presented functionality appears to be consistent with what subjects under deep hypnosis experience. It is also very similar to experiences of remote viewers during a remote viewing session where the remote viewer feels empathy, compassion, and describes "seeing through the eyes" of a victim or target.

In my case during a remote viewing master class, I believe I experienced sensory perceptions related to the physical environment of one of my assigned targets, the planet or minor planet in our solar system named Pluto.

Imprinting

Many subjects under deep hypnosis have reported accessing stored information for study in-between lifetimes. For example, Cannon writes about her experience in client sessions where clients have described using specific recorded information from other souls to prepare for the first incarnation of a school such as the Earth school. "It also has the Akashic Records, which are the records of every life that has ever been lived since the creation. Through much discussion and advice with the Librarian, the soul picks out lifetimes that it wants to be imprinted upon its soul pattern" (Cannon 2011, 11).

The idea of accessing the Divine Library while in-between physical lives to replay and study specific lives or scenarios becomes a very efficient methodology for training. A soul might download the lifetime, or receive a soul book, and experience the entire life by creating an imprint on the soul.

I see how the imprint approach might be perceived as a predestined life experience since free will would not be possible given the soul is only replaying a life that had already been lived.

The alternative to an imprint is to actually experience a similar lifetime. The lifetime would be planned out as a rough sketch with major events and markers. The soul then incarnates and experiences the lifetime dynamically with free will choices and causality impacts.

Spirit Guide Hints

In book one, I discussed the idea of hints and whispers from Spirit Guides to occasionally nudge the incarnated soul during a lifetime. But even the idea of listening to hints and whispers is an incarnated soul choice to listen or not listen.

Integrating Spirit Guide hints into the timeline of moments translates into dynamics illustrated in the figure below. Note the circles with numbers in the diagrams.

Item 1 represents the timeline of moments during a life experience.

Item 2 represents a major life event occurring at the moment t6.

This brings us to item 3, where the soul has a decision to make as the result of unfolding events represented by moment t6.

In the future moment example represented by paths inside the dashed rectangle, there are two possible scenario paths, depending on a decision to be made during the lifetime by the incarnated soul.

Note: since possible paths are in the future, these paths are probability paths dependent upon both the free will decisions made by the soul and countless external events combined with the free will of all other interacting souls who are shaping the unfolding of the scenario.

Focusing specifically on a soul's perspective in the example, choosing a path depends on the decision made by asserting free will to make a decision.

Item 5 represents a path to the moments t7 and t8 where there are no significant preplanned events, whereas item 6 reflects a second possible path to a different set of moments t7 and t8 where a major life event occurs at moment t7.

Physical location is a good example of scenarios that may play an important role in the soul's life experience as well. For example, there may be life events resulting in a decision to move to one city or another. Both life path scenarios are possible. But the path taken depends on the soul's free will choice.

Using these figures, it should be easier to visualize how life scenarios can be dramatically different in one city or another. It is also exciting and challenging, knowing that each of us has choices to make during our lifetimes.

Scenarios, events, and patterns appear to be dynamic based on internal and external choices and actions. The existence of a loose sketch of possible events driven by an incarnated soul's lifetime choices reinforces the idea that there are no wrong decisions. It is also worth considering the potential impact of not making a decision, which is also a free will choice.

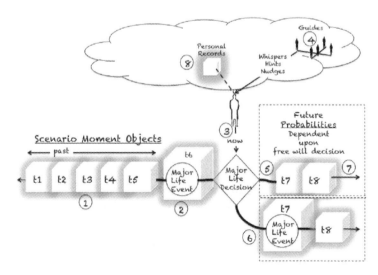

In the above examples and diagrams, the value of trusting intuition and gut instincts to make decisions during the soul's incarnated life journey is highlighted. When intuitions or gut instincts are unclear, asking for heavenly assistance is always my strategy.

I try to remember each of us has free will to make decisions during our lifetime experience. We are empowered to make personal choices. Although, at times it may be frustrating that we do not have all the possible choices we would like to have.

As long as we calm our mind when making decisions and listen to our gut feelings, I believe the choices we make will help us experience life to the fullest. As the Dalai Lama said, "Take into account that great love and great achievements involve great risk."

Perhaps it is also true that there are no wrong decisions, but that does not mean all life paths will be the same nor does it mean the paths we choose will be easy. I know this from my life experience. I learned from the school of hard knocks to trust, listen, and then act when it is time to make a big decision.

This exploration brings me to another question. How do individual life experiences shape the world during our lifetime?

Given my assumption that everything is stored in the Divine Library, and given that we can access our soul book, I recommend we all reach out and try to access the lessons learned from events that have occurred throughout time, moments that have been recorded, and scenarios that have been experienced during incarnated soul lifetimes.

It also makes sense that our previous life experiences have shaped our societies, economies, industries, etc. This idea is important because it means that we incarnated souls have the power to change our world in whatever way we collectively believe is vital to ensure future incarnations are more rewarding, a great learning experience, and involve a limited amount of suffering.

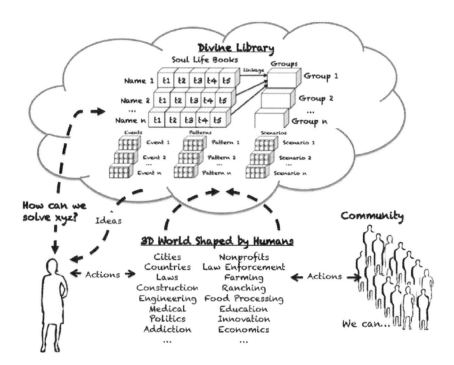

If we embrace that we are incarnated souls experiencing physical life, we should be able to do our best to open our hearts long enough to collectively build the world we wish to live in. We have the power to assert our free will to shape all aspects of our life experience. This includes: economics, the environment, education, medicine, politics, the legal system, and so on.

If you want to push the boundaries, experiment with the Divine Library by requesting information from beyond the Earth soul school. What might we learn about enhancing our life experience? What big problems can we solve by learning how other civilizations solved similar issues millions of years ago?

Perhaps this book and others like it will give readers confidence and determination to push aside ego to work together on comprehensive solutions.

Chapter 8
Meditation, Prayer, and Connecting to Spirit

Reports from hypnotherapy regressions indicate time and time again there exists a spiritual resource referred to as a library and soul life books that are studied and reviewed between lifetimes. Others such as Howe, Chyan, and Ortiz access this divine information, or what they call "Akashic Records," after connecting directly to spiritual realms with a specific prayer. And there is Cayce, who accessed spiritual information while in a trance state.

I wondered if anyone could access the Divine Library?

From my research and life experience of applying prayer and meditation, the answer is yes. Anyone can access the Divine Library and its contents.

Author Linda Howe agrees. She says, "Today anyone with a conscious commitment to seeking and spreading the Divine Light and healing can access this body of wisdom, insight, and guidance" (Howe 2010, 11).

If you have limited experience with prayer, meditation, hypnotherapy, or regression, the next question you will likely ask will be: How do I access the Divine Library?

Many people use deeply personal approaches to prayer and meditation to connect to spiritual realms from their spiritual perspective. Some receive help from a teacher, clinical hypnotherapist, or counselor. Other people turn to third parties who channel personal insights from the Divine Library.

Before specifically discussing Divine Library access, let us take a step back and ponder big events that may have occurred in our lives and the impacts those events have had on our life experience.

Challenging Life Events

Most of us have experienced a life event in the past that prompted us to pray for help or guidance. Challenging life events may include a sudden loss of a loved one, a tragedy, an accident, the loss of a job, or a scenario caused by other circumstances.

In The Isaiah Effect, author Gregg Braden writes about six months of informal surveys asking the following question: "When you pray, what do you find yourself praying about?" Participants from different backgrounds, locations, and ages responded, "more money, better jobs, better health, and better relationships, in precisely that order" (Braden 2000, 146–47).

In a 2014 religious landmark study by Pew Research Center with a sample size of more than 35,000 participants living in every state across the United States: 55 percent pray at least daily, 16 percent weekly, 6 percent monthly, 23 percent seldom or never, 1 percent don't know.

In another 2014 survey, entitled the American Prayer Practices Survey with a sample size of over 1,000, prayer among adult Americans reported the following topics and percentages: family = 82 percent, personal problems or difficulties = 74 percent, good things that occurred recently = 54 percent, victims of natural disasters = 38 percent, future prosperity = 36 percent, government leaders = 12 percent, celebrities and other public figures = 5 percent (LifeWay Research 2014).

As reflected in this small sampling of surveys, most of us pray. It turns out, many of us believe in a higher power or spiritual realms.

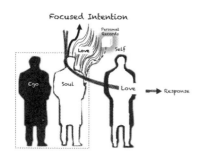
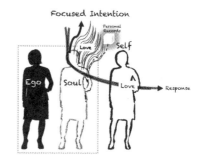

On some past occasions when I used meditation or prayer to seek assistance or guidance from a higher power, I received what I felt were answers. Other times, I felt as if answers took much longer than I had hoped. And occasionally, my prayers were not answered at all or as I had expected.

Reflecting on my life, even when my prayers had not been answered I still did not give up. Instead, I found myself working harder, sometimes on my own, sometimes with the support from a community of loving people, close friends, or relatives around me. Regardless of traditional or nontraditional spiritual beliefs, traditions, processes, sacred books, or sacred rituals, we all have periods in our lives where we search for answers and seek the help of a higher power. From NDE and regression research combined with my personal experiences, I have no doubt there is a divine support system ready and willing to come to my aid when I ask for help.

With my new awareness of the existence of a Divine Library, I extend my requests for guidance to the library and support resources when I need answers. I feel comforted and reassured knowing access to a spiritual library is available to me. Of course, reassurance doesn't necessarily mean life experiences will be easier or that I will receive something specific every time I ask.

Opening up to believe Spirit Guides or other spiritual entities such as deceased loved ones will gently nudge and assist me from time to time throughout my journey gives me confidence.

Remember from earlier chapters, a lack of response or unfulfilled request could be due to the timing being wrong or other events that must occur before my request can be answered. Sometimes I need to remind myself we are here to learn during our physical lifetimes.

Most life experiences require effort, time, and circumstance. But that does not mean I should stop asking questions or accessing information in the Divine Library when life events do not go my way or turn out as I want them to turn out.

Prayer

Occasionally, I wonder if my prayers are too broad or too

focused on a particular outcome. Think about your prayers. If you do pray, how do you pray? Do you ask for something? Do you ask for help to resolve a situation or manage a relationship? Do you wish to help someone else? Do you say thank you?

What if we adjusted our prayers or shifted our meditation to focus our intent on loving guidance? What if we asked for insights and awareness to resolve our problem(s)?

Maybe we should ask for patience to handle a specific situation with love, unselfishness, but with firmness and boundaries, while standing up for ourselves when incarnated souls over- assert their free will in a way that affects our lives negatively.

What if we embellished our prayers with requests for problem-solving ideas to resolve the situation?

Instead of asking for a specific outcome such a job promotion, resolution of a family issue, getting this or that, what if we pray for wisdom and guidance to handle a situation with love and kindness?

Perhaps we can enhance the way we pray by highlighting our feelings. In her book Change Me Prayers, Tosha Silver offers many beautiful prayer examples. Silver says, "The essence of these prayers is surrender. You're inviting the Divine to make changes IT wishes to make" (Silver 2015, 3).

Assuming the Divine Library contains every energy fluctuation and vibration, I am confident answers exist somewhere in the library. In their books, Newton, Cannon, and others have shared hypnotherapy sessions where subjects report observing souls studying in a Divine Library. Studying in a library implies information is available.

However, what if the desired answer affects another soul's life experience or life plan? In other words, what happens when our search for answers is related to relationships with other incarnated souls? What if the particular incarnated soul of interest has a life plan that is different from my life plan? What if events are out of our control and there is nothing that can be done to change the situation?

Remember free will is a double-edged sword. On the one hand, you are free to make decisions during your life. On the other hand, every other incarnated soul living and sharing this moment is free to make decisions about their lives. Free will extends far beyond relationships.

It is easy to get caught up in the drama of life events and let our emotions dictate how we respond to situations. Maybe the best response to difficult situations is a prayer for strength, love, and surrender, trusting that dark clouds in our life will lift and sunny days will return, believing we will have future choices and new exciting learning experiences.

It might be a time for new growth and to experience new places or new relationships. We must trust that difficult life moments will pass and pray or meditate for positive energy and strength.

There are times in all of our lives when it is not easy. But we can work through those times. I know this to be true from my own life experience. It is natural to desire specific outcomes, but maybe my perceived problems are not about "me" at all.

In those stressful situations, our prayers may not be answered in the way we wish. We must rely on our faith. Ask for strength to do the best we can to handle a situation or event with love and an open heart.

That said, I am not suggesting to sit back and have faith spiritual realms will solve our problems or manipulate a given situation for us. We need to remember to pray for answers, guidance, and support.

Ultimately, it is up to us to make difficult decisions or work at resolving a situation or the problems in our life. We are the ones who will need to assert our free will and make decisions to become an active participant in our life experience.

When I encounter a situation where I don't know how to respond, I realize it is the perfect opportunity for a personal prayer of guidance. A "show me how" worded prayer rather than a "solve this for me" prayer.

Meditation

Author Ernesto Ortiz says, "There is no better way to digest and understand the information we receive from the Akashic Records than through meditation" (Ortiz 2015, 95).

The benefits of meditation have been well documented. Meditation starts by focusing on something specific such as breath, clearing one's mind, and achieving an emotionally calm state. Then we observe our thoughts from afar without judgment and free of emotion.

In my interview with Angela Thompson Smith, she said, "An ancient form of meditation that I find helpful is contemplation, focusing on a particular topic without judgment or decision-making, just pondering and observing and keeping focused." Both prayer and meditation shut off the chatter and facilitate calmness. This process of concentration focuses on the present moment while shutting down the mind's chatter experienced during a typical day.

Once this is done through practice and intent, we can journey deeper within ourselves and discover our soul connection to everything around us and on to spiritual realms.

It is a strange concept, setting the ego aside in order to journey deeper within one's self to connect beyond our self.

In his book, Inner Engineering, Yogi Sadhguru Jaggi Vasudev believes going inward changes the pursuit of joy into an expression of joyfulness. Sadhguru says, "If you go outward, it is an endless journey. If you turn inward, it is just one moment" (Vasudev 2016, 39). I love that quote! Although, it is a challenging visual indeed. From my experience, I have found going inward is the only way I can connect to everything outward in spiritual realms.

Reflecting back to book one, recall that I defined Self as consisting of my Ego plus my soul. When our Self intensely focuses on something as subtle as breathing, we distract our Ego long enough to connect with the soul part of our Self. I think about it like how my laptop computer connects to a wireless network, which in turn connects to the Internet.

I can use my laptop computer without such a wireless connection to the Internet; but to access a vast repository of information and applications, I must connect to the network.

Perhaps we are like a laptop computer. Meditation, prayer, or hypnosis are like the wireless network enabling us to connect beyond the laptop.

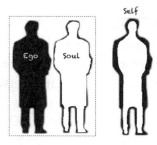

Let's ask another question. Once we quiet our Ego and connect with our soul, are we able to reach spiritual realms beyond our Self? Book one answered this question with a yes.

So where do we reach when we are reaching beyond our Self?

Since I am not connecting with something physical in the three-dimensional world, I must be reaching higher dimensions, that is, spiritual realms, the spirit world, or universal consciousness.

Meditation assists me in connecting beyond my Self. When I reach a meditative state, I open up to receive subtle messages and insights from spiritual realms.

I do not think it matters if one meditates, prays, or just applies focused intention. In my opinion, all that matters is finding what personally works to connect to spiritual realms.

Accessing the Library

The first step to access the Divine Library is by turning off one's conscious mind using meditation, prayer, regression, self-hypnosis, or other means.

All such approaches work with practice, but one method may resonate with you more than the others. The key is to quiet the conscious mind and focus. Concentrate on loving intention.

Once my mind is quiet, I ask specific questions and listen for answers by accessing the Divine Library either directly, through a channel, or with help from my Spirit Guides. Since responses are often very subtle, I must pay close attention and stay open to my intuition and gut feelings. Answers seem to come to me when I least expect them.

Some teachers working directly with the Akashic Records have indicated there are rules and spiritual entities managing access. While I do not doubt their first-hand experience, I think there might be a wide range of approaches, or even a more straightforward approach, to access the Divine Library.

My process is to shape each inquiry I make to the Divine Library into specific terms and focus my intention on love. Then I say a little prayer for help in receiving answers and I open up to whatever I receive.

Chapter 9
Intention and Problem Solving

Have you ever had an idea out of the blue or thought of a solution to a problem that was entirely out of left field? Have you experienced a sudden inspiration for something creative like a song, a painting, a photograph, or a design and wondered where it came from? Many of these types of scenarios occur organically and may be the product of one's natural thought process, imagination, or interests. But I think there is also another source for some of our creative out-of-the-blue ideas. There are also times when I have received a subtle feeling in my gut that came out of the blue. Such feelings have been as simple as "call so-and- so" or as jarring as "take action now." I call those times divine inspiration.

Many of us believe these nudges come from spiritual entities such as a deceased loved one or Spirit Guides who are sending us a sign or communicating with us in a subtle way.

Actions versus Insights

As I continue with my spiritual journey and explore the Divine Library, I wonder if there is a distinction between gut feelings to take action and creative insights. That is, gut feelings to take action may come by way of a gentle spiritual nudge, whereas inspiration may be information received from the Divine Library or indirectly with the help of our Spirit Guides sending information to us by way of intuition, gut feelings, or signs.

As an inventor and creative person, I have often wondered about the origins of some of my out-of-the-blue inspirations and crazy ideas. I asked myself the following questions:

"Did that particular insight come from heavenly guides or a deceased loved one?"

"How did I think of that?"

It does not feel like a stretch to assume many of my inspirations have come from spiritual realms. I find this idea exciting and embrace the belief that spiritual realms are actively part of my daily life. But to really understand how information from the Divine Library can enhance my life experience, I need to dig deeper.

Previous chapters have proposed the concept of linkages from the recorded raw stream of every vibration and energy fluctuation to a particular soul book or group book. What if those linkages included a wide range of life experience events, special moments, or other useful information stored in the form of inspirations?

Instead of limiting questions to answers from only my soul lifetime records, what if I could access and learn from another soul's inspirational life experiences? What if a subset of moments related to specific lessons and inspirations could be made available for my soul to access?

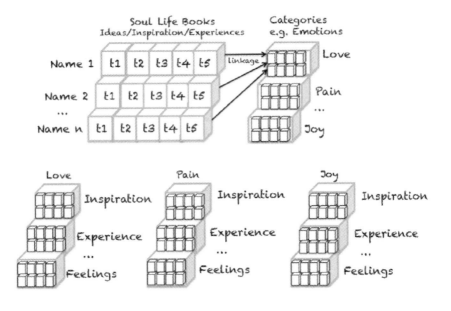

As presented in earlier chapters, perhaps the information in the Divine Library is categorized in such a way that allows souls to receive insights from general events experienced by other souls. To further explain this idea and the logic behind it, assume the concept of linkages is combined with the belief that some inspirations come from spiritual realms, deceased loved ones, or guides.

Extrapolating this idea leads to a new assertion that some select information in the Divine Library might be diced and sliced for the benefit of another soul to learn from it. I am not talking about life experience events that might be essential to the growth of the specific soul who experienced it. Rather, I am referring to events that might provide a more general impact for another soul such as creating a piece of music for the first time, realizing what it feels like to paint a scene, or dreaming up an invention that solves a problem.

With this idea in mind, categories of specific events could be linked from individual soul records and be made available to another soul with a need or desire to access the event from the Divine Library. A soul, or the soul's Spirit Guide, could then request a category of life experiences that had been previously recorded by other souls.

The request might then prompt a response from the Divine Library, Spirit Guides, or record keepers and be received by the inquiring soul or soul in need, assuming the soul is ready for the information.

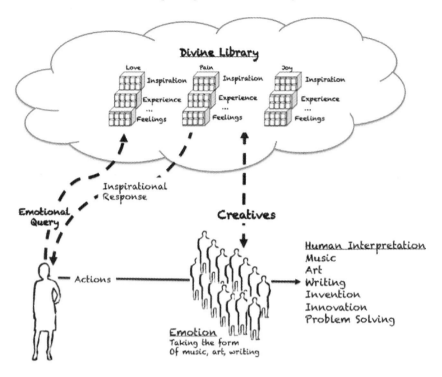

Incarnated souls who receive responses must then apply their interpretation and life experience to the response, which may result in inspired music, art, writings, inventions, innovations, and other creations.

As we experience emotion and receive inspiration, the process feels natural. But what about making specific inquiries with focused intent and asking for divine inspiration?

How can we get better at making requests of the Divine Library and practicing the process enough to recognize the difference between heavenly inspiration and our brain's natural informational processing and imagination?

Visualization

If I visualize where my questions go, I believe it becomes possible to shape questions in such a way as to receive the specific answers I am seeking.

Given that I am discussing higher dimensions, it may even

turn out that by visualizing the Divine Library, we are organizing access and enhancing our ability to receive specific information from within the Divine Library.

Angela Thompson Smith compares this approach to remote viewing. She says, "This is similar to tasking in remote viewing; a great project can be ruined by inadequate tasking that is not specific enough. Tasking a project is as important as the viewing."

This exploration of the Divine Library illustrates the importance of prayer and meditation with focused intention and love as an approach to access the Divine Library. Of course, we have also learned that timing plays a crucial role in the process of when such requests can receive responses.

Perhaps the way to visualize this process is to visualize our inquiry as the key to unlocking access to the Divine Library, but the lock also includes a valid need and a timing mechanism that must align with timing in our three-dimensional physical world before answers can be received.

Divine Library responses may use an algorithm such as: Inquiry + Timing + Need = Divine Library Access and Response.

If timing is essential, how do I know when to make inquiries? I think the best approach to address this concern is not to worry about timing. Send the question out there. Then contemplate timing as the reason you may not receive a response as quickly as desired.

Process

Dissecting the process into manageable steps may assist in the understanding of the process. By embracing each step, we can incorporate the steps into our prayers and meditation as illustrated by the following flow chart:

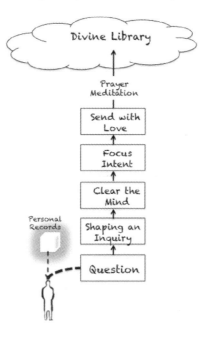

As discussed, I usually start with a little prayer describing my intention. Sometimes I meditate to calm my mind then focus on intention. You decide what works for you.

When I feel ready, I form a question in my mind and shape it into a specific inquiry, which means transforming the request into words to describe my intention. Then I clear my mind of everything except for the request and focus intently on it. I add feelings of love, reminding myself of my intention and heartfelt desire for answers and solutions.

Finally, I pray or meditate to send off the inquiry to spiritual realms believing in my heart there is spiritual support ready to receive my request and allow me to obtain the desired information from the Divine Library.

Shaping words into specific questions that reflect an emotional situation can be a challenge given our earthly language limitations. I typically try to combine my question with a description of the emotions behind the request when I ask for assistance from the Divine Library. In the next chapter, I explore a strategy for forming questions while contemplating what NDErs tell us upon returning to earthly life after their first-hand experience of spiritual realms.

Chapter 10
Compiling Questions

Before attempting to craft questions, it is essential to step back and reflect on what is most important about personal life experiences. What do NDErs say about life experiences upon returning to their earthly lives after experiencing spiritual realms? From the vast amount of available research, many NDErs return to their life experiences with a new outlook on life. NDErs often make significant changes to their lives, reprioritizing the importance of money and the value of material items. Other changes reported by NDErs include deeper feelings of compassion for others, understanding the importance of kindness, and a more profound sense of love.

Two excellent NDE sources provide information related to thousands of NDEs. These sources include The Handbook of Near-Death Experiences: Thirty Years of Investigation and The International Association of Near Death Experiences (IANDS). https://iands.org/.

In The Handbook of Near-Death Experiences, researchers summarize reports related to NDErs life perspective changes and priorities. Some of these include

- ○ Loss of fear of death
- ○ Strengthened belief in life after death
- ○ A new sense of purpose or divine mission, even when it is unclear what the mission is supposed to be
- ○ Increased compassion and love for others
- ○ Lessened concern for material gain
- ○ Greater desire to serve others

- ○ Increased ability to express feelings
- ○ Greater appreciation of life and a zest for life
- ○ Increased focus on the present moment
- ○ Deeper spiritual faith—heightened spirituality
- ○ Search for deeper knowledge
- ○ Greater appreciation for nature (J. M. Holden et al. 2009, 45–46)

From my research, I have also found perspective changes among many subjects who experienced one or more past-life regressions or between-life regressions. I can also confirm my own personal perspective changes after first-hand experiences with regressions and hypnotherapy.

With this information in mind, it is important to ask the following questions in preparation for making inquiries to the Divine Library:

- ▶ Am I asking a question related to material or relationship want or is it a desire to enhance life experience for me or someone else?
- ▶ Am I asking a question with a want to change a situation for whatever reasons or is my question a desire to grow and open up my heart to learn something new?

It can be challenging to put our self-centered egos in a time-out while we experience life in a loving and caring way. But a full life cannot be experienced without our egos. In other words, to experience physical life, it requires *Ego + Soul = Self.*

That means Ego is an active part of our life experience. The value of knowing that we consist of ego and soul makes it easier to evaluate our internal feelings during life events and the decision-making process. This awareness can give us a moment to pause and consider how to respond, how we will react to a particular situation, word choice, and emotion.

I do not believe there is anything "wrong" or "incorrect"

by asking questions involving emotional wants or desires. But the challenge can come into play when our wants and desires are so strong they affect our ability to receive unfiltered information, or information that is not tainted by our desire for a certain response.

I try to apply this philosophy to the way I respond to events in my life. I do my best to take a second or two and think before taking action. I try to hold my tongue and ask myself: is my desire to respond in a certain way coming from ego or the soul part of my self? Granted, it can be difficult to take a moment before replying when emotions intensify.

However, we can be spiritual while embracing our physical life experience and working toward economic or career goals. For example, it is possible to be a loving and caring person while running a demanding business, working at a job, trying to get promoted, or going to school to obtain a degree in our earthly economic and social environment.

Each of us has an incredible opportunity to learn with so many other incarnated souls in a wide variety of diverse roles as we experience life in this grand Earth school. We need business leaders, teachers, mechanics, animal rescuers, engineers, spiritual teachers, the spiritual student, and so on.

Such a diverse range of learning experience opportunities is one reason why many hypnotherapists, including Cannon and Newton, have said this Earth school for souls is so demanding.

Crafting Questions

With these ideas in mind, it is important to point out that it is possible for us to collectively change the social environment, geopolitical structure, and economic structure to shape our Earth school to be a more loving and caring school for learning.

Having established the rationale that information in the Divine Library contains both soul books and cross-referenced linkage to provide general information, I have come to believe our questions can extend beyond the physical lives we have experienced.

Let us explore some possible inquiries we may wish to make of the Divine Library's vast repositories. For example, looking around the world today, there are millions of people suffering every year from disease, lack of water, and lack of food. Inquiries to the Divine Library might include requests such as the following:

Please show me how to use technology to bring water to town [insert name here].

Help me understand the purpose of the mosquito and show me how I might protect human life from disease-carrying mosquitos.

Of course, this may require learning a great deal of technical information before we can understand the answer. The response might be an inspiration to take classes such that our questions can become more technical and refined, such as the following:

Help me understand how to separate air molecules such that I can farm water from the air.

Help me understand how the mosquito fits into the ecosystem and what would happen without it.

Questions become more detailed as we understand more. In fact, I sometimes find heavenly responses arriving by way of interests and inspirations in related topics. The process may cause me to ask more and more questions until I discover a newly inspired desire to do something in a new way.

This process has helped me understand the value of cross-referencing technologies from entirely different or unrelated fields to solve problems. Eventually, additional knowledge may provide a solution to a specific problem.

Throughout the process, a whole host of unintended problems may be solved, other people may be inspired to solve problems, and I most likely will have learned a great deal.

Solutions

I have had ah-ha moments when a problem's solution comes to me in a burst. But more often than not I must work at understanding what is at the core of my questions to fully appreciate the problem(s) I want to solve.

Some may believe this process of trial, error, and question refinement is merely a natural problem-solving process. I must say that in many ways that could be true. But what if I embellish the process and explicitly ask for assistance from spiritual realms? What if love and inspiration fill me with excitement and passion for making life better when I ask for divine help?

Perhaps by combining our natural abilities with my connection to spiritual realms, we can discover more loving, caring, and thoughtful solutions to problems. Maybe this entire process is a form of brainstorming with spiritual realms.

Brainstorming with Spiritual Realms

The first step in brainstorming is getting into the practice of keeping notes in a journal or notebook. A written record enables periodic reflection on the questions you asked and the thoughts that came to you. It is also a good idea to include dates. I do this to get a high-level perspective by reviewing my notes while I brainstorm.

It is fascinating to look over prior months and see how much growth has occurred and how my questions change. I like to review the types of questions I have asked in the past and how I felt about those questions at the time.

It is hard to think clearly when emotions or excitement overwhelm us. Keeping a notebook or journal is a great way to peer through feelings that may be clouding decision- making abilities or concealing possible choices.

I applied a similar brainstorming process as I wrote this book. When I became stuck while writing, I said a little prayer for insights then asked more questions. I gave my questions time to brew as I processed my thoughts, feelings, and reviewed references and sources.

Often, I found myself sketching out diagrams and writing down thoughts and research notes. I surprised myself many times with how much information flowed to me. It was interesting how new insights showed up in my mind when I became stuck. Each new idea felt essential to note and research further.

Below is a summary of my process. Give it a try. Adjust the process below to fit your style and what resonates with you. It is important for the entire process to feel natural.

✓ Use a notepad or a word processor on a computer
✓ Write down questions

✓ Clear your mind and fill it with love and compassion

✓ Let ideas flow into your mind
✓ Sketch out or write notes about the things that come to you

✓ Pay particular attention to how the incoming thoughts make you feel.

✓ How do the ideas make you feel?

Most of the above steps have been my brainstorming process for many years as I have developed innovations and technology. The only steps I have added to the process include filling my mind with love and compassion, then being mindful of how I feel about the ideas and thoughts that come to me.

Reflecting on past approaches to innovation and brainstorming, I had been much more analytical and did not think about feelings or divine inspiration. Instead, I was problem solving and actively working at the moment. The addition of adding emotion and loving feelings to my approach made my insights and discoveries more profound and more exciting.

I have had excellent results when framing questions with a preamble or description of why I am asking a particular question. I do this primarily to clarify the problem and make the request specific.

For example, I write something like the following in my notebook and shape it into a prayer: I am passionate about helping others who seek answers to questions about life purpose and enhancing the life experience. Please show me how to access general information stored in higher dimensions that will provide solutions and support for all souls.

With this sort of an inquiry, I do not intend to make it personal or describe my specific journey. I hope for a general response that enables me to articulate important features of the Divine Library to assist readers to visualize categories of data that might be in the response that is received.

A couple of days after asking questions, new ideas arrived. One such example is when I became very excited about the idea of Divine Library raw data linkages. The idea seemed to come out of nowhere. The concept felt as if it solved the problem I had visualized about massive duplication of data.

This may sound convenient, and it is true that I do understand how such database linkages work in earthly technology and repositories. Nevertheless, the insight of applying linkage functionality to my description of the Divine Library was unexpected and worked nicely.

The linkage idea response I had received motivated me to leverage the idea into new diagrams to visualize it, showing segments of incarnated soul lifetime experience moments stored in many soul books all linked to form more general lessons and inspirations resulting from those linkages.

And just like that, I visualized the following image, which I sketched out in my notebook:

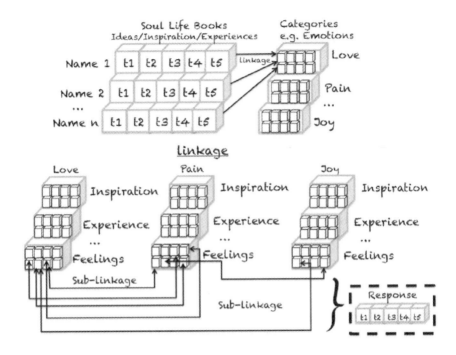

The linkages relate back to a particular soul life experience but are not specific to a soul, which might be considered personal or private to a particular soul. Categories such as love, pain, and joy could exist in volumes and be available for a soul to study those specific experiences in- between lifetimes.

With information available, it seems reasonable to assume categories of data are available to us by merely asking the right question and visualizing answers coming from within the Divine Library. For example, when asking why there is so much suffering in the world, the above experience linkages could be combined and shaped into a personal response that provides insights and inspiration to the incarnated soul who asks the question.

In the next chapter, I explore how to interpret responses from the Divine Library.

Chapter 11
Interpreting Responses

To receive information from the Divine Library, I have found there to be at least four primary approaches to do so. These approaches are as follows:

1. Direct access to the Divine Library using prayer or meditation to initiate the connection, define intention, and ask the question or make the inquiry.

2. Ask Spirit Guides or other spiritual entities to assist by accessing the Divine Library to answer questions, then sending responses by way of feelings, intuition, images, and thoughts.

3. By way of hypnotherapy where a hypnotherapist asks the subject under deep hypnosis to go to the library and ask questions to be answered with information from the Divine Library.

4. Obtain assistance from a third party with the ability to access Divine Library information and channel reading of the records like Cayce as discussed in earlier chapters.

Direct Access

Spiritual teacher and author Ernest Ortiz says once information has been requested from the Akashic Records the next step is to receive information from the records. The requestor opens up to receive energy and allows an inflow of information, then applies his or her senses to decode and write down the received information (Ortiz 2015, 134–35).

Authors Jacki Smith and Patty Shaw write in their book, Do It Yourself Akashic Wisdom, "As you visit your records more and more, you will begin to notice a rhythm to your healing" (Smith and Shaw 2013, 202).

Spirit Guides and Deceased Loved Ones

While many experts and spiritual teachers speak of communication with Spirit Guides, research suggests millions of people believe answers and assistance may come from deceased loved ones.

Researchers Bill Guggenheim and Judy Guggenheim created The ADC Project in 1988. These researchers conducted in-depth research of After-Death Communications (ADC), including interviews of 2,000 people from all fifty American states and ten Canadian provinces and collected over 3,300 first-hand accounts from people who believe they had been contacted by a loved one who had died. The ADC Project website states, "It is estimated that 60–120 million Americans—20–40% of the population of the United States—have had one or more ADC experiences" (ADC Project). In Hello from Heaven! the authors include over 350 first-hand accounts of people who report having received messages or signs from the deceased (Guggenheim and Guggenheim 1995).

Hypnotherapy

Hypnotherapists Cannon, De Tamble, Newton, Tomlison, Weiss, and many others describe insights from sessions with subjects, suggesting spiritual entities such as Spirit Guides communicate with their subjects during day-to-day life experience by way of intuition, gut feelings, and thought.

Weiss says of his subjects, "Others have mediumistic abilities, the capacity to receive and to transmit messages and knowledge from beings 'on the other side'" (Weiss 2000, 188).

In one session with a subject, Newton writes, "Her Spirit Guide is represented by the gut feeling and instincts that she has been experiencing all this time" (Newton 2009, 291).

Hypnotherapist Scott Fitzgerald De Tamble says he assists subjects during sessions in becoming more aware of the whispers coming from Spirit Guides during the client's daily life (De Tamble 2018).

Revisiting Intuition, Gut Feelings, Whispers

Many of us ask the question: How can I tell the difference between a typical thought process and something beyond myself such as whispers from Spirit Guides or deceased loved ones?

The challenge is that most responses and messages from spiritual realms are often subtle and hard to tell apart from the thoughts that come from our creative minds during a typical day.

Many of us believe we have had moments where intuition tells us to take an unexpected action that turns out to help us avoid something bad that "could have" affected our life experience. It can be difficult to discuss it. Or when we do try to explain the exact spiritual scenario that had occurred, the friend or family member listening does not grasp the significance.

I have experienced what I felt was Spirit Guide intervention and assistance. I have also received what I thought to be messages from deceased loved ones.

Some medical experts may describe the notion of heavenly whispers, intuition, or gut feelings as our imagination or answers we hope to receive. Regardless of what others say, I cherish my personal experiences receiving what I believe to be heavenly support.

In the moment of each occurrence, I felt the experience to be a divine message or a sign from spiritual realms. The experience was my first-hand experience and the way I interpreted how I felt in that moment.

I have also had first-hand experiences where I felt messages came from deceased loved ones, out-of-the-blue intuitive moments, and even dreams that I chose to interpret as support from spiritual realms.

Skeptics can say what they wish, but it will not change what I experienced and how I felt. I trust gut feelings and take action when I think I should do so. It is always a personal choice. Scenarios can include insignificant moments like song lyrics playing over and over in my head with words that do not go away until I finally understand the message.

Significant life-changing moments have occurred during my life where I chose to act. Later, I felt my actions helped me to avoid something that could have done me harm.

Was it instinct? Heavenly guidance? You decide for yourself from your first-hand life experience.

Channels

Using a channel or a teacher to connect to the Divine Library is another approach to access one's soul records. Edgar Cayce is an excellent example of a third party who accessed the Akashic Records to provide information for his clients. His process evolved over his lifetime, involving a sleep-like trance where he would focus on healing individuals in need or providing them with answers on any topic or question they asked. Today there are many who offer channeling services to give readings for clients.

Personal Choice

Choosing a method to connect spiritually and seek information from spiritual realms is a very personal choice. The process of exploring spiritual connections must personally resonate. You decide which is the best approach for you.

The only suggestion I would add from my experience is to make sure you decide how to interpret the messages you receive. Trust your intuition and gut feelings.

Spiritual Support

Spiritual assistance is not only available, it is persistent. It seems to me our Spirit Guides can be steadfast in a pursuit to provide us with the needed support. Even when I had closed off myself to the possibility of spiritual guidance, Spirit Guides, or spiritual entities, divine messages used other routes to get my attention.

A great example of steadfast Spirit Guide support in my life is the significant life moment when I nearly died from a pulmonary embolism (PE). I refer to this example because the experience for me was too significant to argue away as coincidence or dumb luck. You decide for yourself if you agree as I reflect back on my experience and step through the critical events of that day once again. Here is a summary:

Moment One

I woke up feeling terrible, but I was determined to attend a meeting with a big customer that was too important (in my mind) to cancel. My wife noticed my coloring was off right away and asked me how I felt. I told her I felt okay and downplayed it. After all, I had to push on to attend that meeting I told myself. She told me I needed to go to the ER. I brushed it off.

Moment Two

As I was persistent about going to work, my wife remained determined that I go to the ER. She demanded I listen to her. Mind you, I have a hard head, but our love for each other trumped everything. I listened.

Moment Three

We went to the hospital where the busy ER doctors could not figure out what was going on with me. They ran all the heart tests they could think to run, but still could not determine what was wrong. Perhaps it was just angina or something else, they mused. My heartbeat was erratic and my coloring was turning grayer by the moment. My oxygen levels had fallen. It seemed my body was shutting down. The doctors could not figure out why.

Moment Four

The ER had become busy. The doctors felt I had stabilized. They moved me into the hallway, but I was not getting any better. My wife noticed my coloring had become worse. When she asked me how I felt, I told her I was exhausted. She knew whatever was wrong with me was getting worse. Again, my wife took action. She told the nurses of her concerns, who in turn communicated with the ER doctors. I was put back into an ER room for more tests, but nothing showed up.

Moment Five

A young intern showed up for her shift. She took a look at my chart and was puzzled too. But this time the intern persisted. Something prompted her to ask the most important question of my life: "Has anyone done a Spiral CT scan on Mr. Rowe?"

Moment Six

The Spiral CT scan revealed a pulmonary embolism. From that moment forward, the doctors knew exactly what to do and took action.

Reflecting

I could go back to each of those key moments and tell myself I was lucky or the ER protocol would have eventually figured out what was wrong with me. However, the actions of my wife came from her intuition.

She trusted her gut feelings and remained persistent to find answers. So did the young intern. What had prompted the intern to ask that question at that moment? Luck? Protocol? Was it a process of symptom elimination or troubleshooting regarding searching for the cause of my physical condition?

For some reason, my intuition was clouded on that day by my desire to push through and show up at a critical work meeting, which I felt was necessary for my career. As my condition worsened, my intuition had become clouded by my physical health. Looking back, I can see it took the intuition of others who acted on their gut feelings to save my life. I participated in the process too by listening to my wife and going to the ER.

My life changed forever on that day. I am alive to tell the tale thanks to the intuition and persistence of my wife and a young doctor with a passion for solving medical mysteries and saving people.

Lessons Learned from the Experience

The way I tend to tell the difference between my own internal chatter and heavenly whispers or intuition is by merely trusting my reaction to the feeling. For me, it is a simple and quick test. I ask: How does the thought I just received make me feel?

Whatever the situation, if I trust that the action I want to take does not cause physical harm to someone or is not coming from a selfish, ego-driven place inside of me, I trust the gut feeling and act upon it.

From life experience, I know the feeling when my ego makes demands versus when I feel a loving message originating from spiritual realms.

Through research and experience, I have not found a definitive method to tell the difference between communication with Spirit Guides and my creative mind. It often takes reflection to confirm such a difference exists.

Given the lack of clarity in the moment, I often use a process to access my gut feelings. I ask myself: Is my ego making a demand that I do something or act a certain way with selfish motives or not? It is difficult to know the choice to make when one's feelings and thoughts are confused.

It is worth taking a quick survey of your feelings to try and determine if the desired actions are selfish or coming from a heavenly connection.

Spiritual teacher Jennifer O'Neill says Spirit Guides communicate using telepathy, blocks of thought, a knowing, dreams, and meditation (O'Neill 2012, 19).

Spiritual teacher and author James Van Praagh in his book, *Wisdom from Your Spirit Guides: A Handbook to Contact Your Soul's Greatest Teachers*, writes, "In my workshops, I have students do an exercise to surrender their egos and allow a guide of theirs to come through, either visually or through writing" (Van Praagh 2017, 32, 38–39).

Overthinking by everyone during the medical event described above would have had an adverse outcome for me. I would have died. Statistical estimates suggest that 60,000–100,000 Americans die of DVT/PE each year; 10 to 30 percent of people will die within one month of diagnosis. Sudden death is the first symptom in about one-quarter (25 percent) of people who have a PE (US Department of Health and Human Services, n.d.).

Was I lucky?

I choose to believe it was more than luck that saved my life that day. Spirit Guides, deceased loved ones, or heavenly entities were persistent. They appeared to use other incarnated souls to get the message out to the one in need.

Until I find a reliable way to know the difference between whispers from spiritual realms and my own mind's chatter, I plan on merely trusting my intuition. Perhaps in doing so, I will eventually learn new approaches to determine the difference.

The Process

The following figure illustrates the process of accessing sequences of moments from the Divine Library. It shows the experiences of spiritual teachers who teach students how to directly access the Divine Library (i.e., the soul specific or Akashic Records information in the library) and the first-hand experiences of those aware of subtle suggestions coming from Spirit Guides.

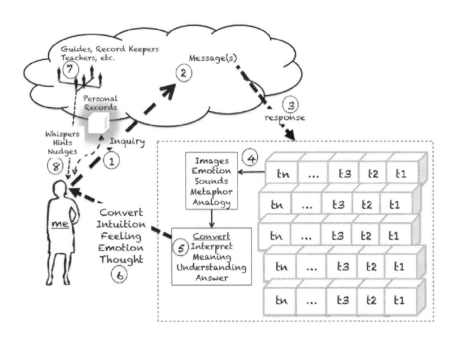

Steps 1 and 2 begin the process by meditating or saying a prayer to ask for assistance, then clearing the mind and focusing in on a specific question to be answered.

Your inquiry must be specific and precise. Also be clear asking for Spirit Guide help to answer and interpret the desired question or requesting to receive information directly from the Divine Library. Personally, I tend to ask for help from Spirit Guides to retrieve answers rather than accessing the Divine Library directly.

Steps 3 and 4 relate to receiving a response. As discussed earlier in this chapter, the response may be very subtle such as a sequence of moments formed into a random thought, a series of images, a gut feeling, a sign, or intuition. The response may come by way of images, emotions, metaphor, or analogy.

The uncertainty part of the process is where many people get frustrated in thinking that a response will come to them when they want it. However, in our physical world driven by timing, answers may not arrive right away.

In steps 5 and 6, it is essential to use any images, thoughts, feelings, or emotions to interpret the answer. The way I do this is by reflecting on the information I receive. I use pen and paper to sketch out the ideas and images, write in a diary, or open up a word processor and type out my thoughts.

I write or sketch whatever comes to me just like I have done for this book. Sometimes I start by drawing images or sketches then write a narrative to describe the images.

I enjoy the process. It is exciting to let my mind drift and think out of the box. I try to remember that whatever I write, I can decide later to keep the raw information flow, edit, or delete it. With an edit process in mind, I feel empowered to be open to recording all ideas and subtle messages.

As a second step, I ask myself how I feel about what I wrote or sketched. Sometimes I discover more answers in my feelings. I write those down too.

Do I feel excited? Do I feel off balance? Is my stomach sinking? Are goose bumps flowing across my shoulders? I may need to rethink my question, asking is the question ego- based or loving?

Why do I need the answer? Sometimes I realize it is time to craft a new question or refine the one I asked.

Stay confident. When the timing is right, you will receive a response. Trust the process. Steps 7 and 8 ask for assistance in interpreting the response.

Say a little prayer or meditate. Ask for guidance in understanding and comprehending the answer(s) to your inquiries.

Some may tell you that what you are doing is using your mind to solve the problems you are asking.

Ultimately, it is up to you to decide if the responses to your questions have come from beyond your Self or from your creative mind. If the answers you receive make your life better or the life experience of someone else better, does it matter where the answers come from?

Personally, I choose to believe in my connection with spiritual realms. It makes life more vibrant and more exciting knowing I have a heavenly support system. All I need to do is ask for help then be patient and stay open to receiving answers.

Chapter 12
Life Purpose

I started this book with an idea of exploring themes such as finding one's purpose. After having established the Divine Library as a resource to search for heavenly answers to important questions, this chapter circles back and uses the Divine Library to search for information about life purpose.

Most people have asked, "What is my purpose?"

I asked this question when major life events motivated me to take some time to reflect and search for answers. In The Book of Joy, writer Douglas Abrams asks the Dalai Lama how it is possible to experience joy even during times of suffering and diversity. The Dalai Lama replied, "There is a Tibetan saying that adversities can turn into good opportunities" (Abrams et al. 2016, 145).

Major Life Events

A significant life event can be the perfect opportunity to ask big questions and evaluate life. An event can be anything that shakes our life experience to its core. This may be a relationship change, a loss of a job, a job situation, a tragic family event, a loss of someone close, a health problem, or any number of other events.

Whatever the scenario, asking what is my purpose usually comes along with waves of emotion, confusion, and an off-balance feeling. It makes sense that a significant life incident would be what it takes to push us out of our comfort zone into a place where asking big questions becomes easier.

Without difficult moments occurring in our lives, we tend to get comfortable and keep moving without asking questions about our life experience.

Given existing economic and social systems that frame our experience and focus our time, moving forward without asking deep questions makes sense. After all, we establish routines. Life feels comfortable. We feel balanced.

We get up, go to work, maybe raise a family, interact with friends and family, and so on. Who has time to ask big questions about the meaning of life or life purpose? We are too busy. Right?

But when a major life-changing event occurs like divorce, loss of a job, or sudden loss of a loved one, our perspective suddenly changes and big questions come into focus and dominate our thoughts. A question starting with "why" is what launched me on the spiritual journey memorialized in my first book. "Why is there so much suffering in the world?" Eventually, my second question became more detailed and personal. "What is my purpose?"

After a significant life event occurs, we often find ourselves struggling to get through the day. Days feel long. We might feel physically sick, off balance, disoriented, confused, emotional, or all the above.

I know this to be true from numerous events that have occurred during my lifetime. When such events have happened to me, everything in my life became difficult. During that time, dealing with day-to-day activities was a struggle. I remember how hard it felt in those moments.

It was a time for me to take a deep breath and open up to getting support from friends, family, and a good counselor.

I was pleasantly surprised. People closest to me wanted to help. Advise came in from all directions.

Once I opened up to new possibilities, I discovered a tremendous amount of support and love. But the process of working through issues took time. I think it is essential during such times to take the time to ask profound questions.

Years ago, I struggled to find balance after one such life event. During that time, I decided to take out my camera and hike the Sierra Nevada Mountains. I used black-and-white film to photograph scenery and wildlife then spent time in my darkroom developing negatives like the one below. The particular photograph is of a very old bristlecone pine, which I admired as I camped and ate fish for dinner caught from a nearby lake.

I kept myself busy, spending time hiking across mountaintops, thinking about spiritual realms, and evaluating my life. At the time, I had no idea what questions to ask or even what I was doing. I just kept myself busy. I forced myself to remain open to learn new things.

I learned what was important to me. For the first time, I thought deeply about spirituality and my connection to higher dimensions. I also learned another valuable lesson about not rushing the growing process. Looking back, when I did rush it at times, I made a few left turns until finally finding my present life path.

It was not easy. I discovered personal growth to be uncomfortable at times. I often forced myself to put one foot in front of the other. I did it.

Looking back, it was a fantastic time of spiritual discovery, and I am thankful for those experiences. I have some pretty cool black-and-white photos of the Sierra Nevada Mountains too.

But I am not unique.

Most of us go through difficult times like these in our lives. Each one of us must learn how to deal with stress and unsteady feelings in ways that are deeply personal.

No matter what your situation, remember first and foremost you are loved, you are special, and you are living this life for a reason. Trust these words to be true even when you want to disagree or lack confidence to see yourself as special.

From my research, I am convinced we all have a purpose. Maybe even more than one purpose. We are all learning lessons and experiencing life.

It is merely a moment in time after a significant life event—a period of uncertainty. In fact, if you are questioning your purpose as you read this book, take the first step to talk with someone like a counselor or dear friend. I promise you that someday you will look back like I am doing now and you will be thankful for the experience.

There is a possibility that significant life events happen at particular moments in time because it allows us opportunities to grow, reevaluate life paths, or discover life purpose. Major life events may be orchestrated by our higher self, soul, or loving spiritual entities such as our Spiritual Guides.

Believe me when I tell you the dark clouds in your life WILL lift and the sun WILL come out. It may also become a moment to ask the question, what is my purpose?

Where Do I Start?

There are many self-help books, websites, and other literature that write about finding one's life purpose. Most say: do what you love, think about who you wish to help, think about what excites you, and so on.

I agree with all those suggestions. But I have asked myself in the past where do I start when I do not know what I love or want to do?

Try the following quick assessment. I came up with the approach as a fun way to get my mind engaged. It is not intended to provide a definitive answer about what you should be doing, but it will hopefully provide a starting point to figure out what feels exciting to you.

It is important to think about the possibility that we all have many purposes throughout our lives. For example, being a teacher, writer, or small business owner. Many of us have changed careers during our lifetime. Sometimes jobs are aligned with purpose; some positions may simply help pay the bills.

For the following fun exercise, complete each item before reading further. Try not to overthink the details on each list as you write down your thoughts.

Keep your mind open. Quickly write down whatever comes to mind. Do not stress about the following lists. Do not overthink or edit your thoughts. This is intended merely to be fun and perhaps thought-provoking.

Exercise

Write down three things on paper for each list as quickly as you can.

Do not overthink any of the following.

List 1. Make a list of things I like to do.
List 2. If you could have any job in the world what would it be?
List 3. What are my current hobbies?
List 4. What gets me upset?
List 5. What makes me laugh?
List 6. The last time I was late for something, I was doing this.

Now take your lists and put an asterisk next to the one item in each of the lists that is the top item of that list. For example, in list one, which one of the three things you wrote down do you like to do best? Circle it.

Use the circled item from each list to fill in the following sentence:

I would like to do [List1] while working as a [List2] and doing [List3] during my free time, but I want to avoid [List4] and laugh while [List5] as long as I am not [List6] because I will be late. Here is an example of how this might look:

Brainstorming Purpose

List 1	List 2	List 3
write	*hypnotherapist	*hiking
*Research	writer	Taking pictures
Play guitar	photographer	traveling

List 4	List 5	List 6
bad customer service	*Playing with the grandkids	*writing
*Red Tape	Playing with golden retriever	self hypnosis
Wasting time	Being a klutz	reading
		watching a movie

Fill in the blanks

I would like to do [List1] while working as a [List2] and doing [List3] during my free time, but I want to avoid [List4] and laugh while [List5] as long as I am not [List6] because I will be late.

I would like to do **RESEARCH** while working as a **HYPNOTHERAPIST** and doing **HIKING** during my free time, but I want to avoid **Red Tape** and laugh while **PLAYING WITH THE GRANDKIDS** as long as I am not **WRITING** because I will be late.

Reinventing Yourself

When I have gone through difficult moments in my life, I needed to force myself out of my comfort zone to stay moving. If you find yourself in this sort of situation, you might consider taking a class on a topic you have always wanted to learn. Join a club. Try new activities. Push yourself to meet new people. Trust that you will find answers to your questions.

To move forward, I believe you must actively stay open to possibilities and open up to receive them. I know from experience it is possible to find personal truth and the happiness that comes with it. But we may need to put in the time and do the work to discover it.

How do I know? you ask. I know this to be true from my life experience. I found my answers. I discovered my truth. So can you.

My first reaction was to close off to the world, but I took a moment and searched my gut. *Is it my ego calling the shots?* I asked myself. *Am I allowing my soul to connect to spiritual realms in this moment?*

Meditate. Pray. Focus.

Do whatever feels comfortable to feel connected beyond your self to higher dimensions or spiritual realms. You may not believe it during difficult times, but trust me—you are loved, and you will find purpose. Answers will arrive at the right time. Stay open and keep moving forward with an open heart.

Life Planning

In Newton's, Tomlison's, and Cannon's books, they discuss experiences with subjects under deep hypnosis who talk about life planning and purpose as illustrated in the diagram below.

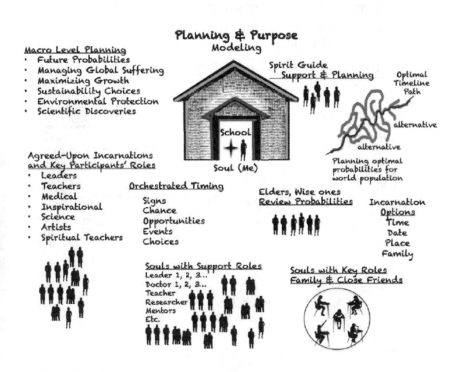

Maybe our current way of thinking about life planning is only one aspect of what is going on. What if we are given numerous choices during our life experience, many purposeful moments, and many key events that occur throughout our lifetime?

Milestones may act as road markers and possible pathways.

Road markers and paths are possibly the only things in our life plan that are predestined.

Perhaps the majority of our life experience is made up of moments where we are empowered to make choices by asserting our free will or by being impacted (positively and negatively) by the free will of the other incarnated souls around us.

I had always assumed there to be only one primary life purpose per incarnated soul, one chance to find a soul mate or one life path. But after a great deal of life experience, research, and thought, I do not believe that anymore.

What if there are different purposes, depending on the readiness of the incarnated soul during a lifetime? Or maybe there is a broader purpose and the incarnated soul works in careers during their lifetime aligned with a more general life purpose.

The following diagram illustrates an example of challenging moments during a period of a lifetime between time n1 and time n2.

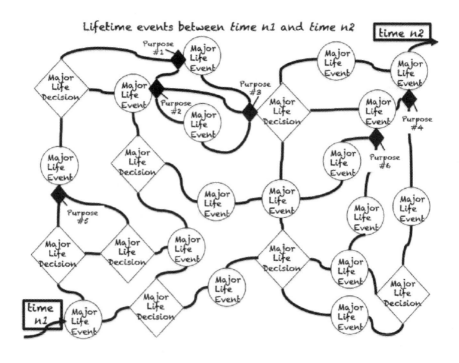

For example, the incarnated soul may focus on teaching

children for the first twenty years of a career, then a significant event occurs later in life, and the incarnated soul changes their job to a mental health care professional.

Was the second career aligned with a more general life purpose such as healing and assisting incarnated souls? The first career dealt with teaching young children in a schooling environment. The second job helped adults. Both professions appear to share a common purpose of supporting incarnated souls.

Or perhaps souls are given the opportunity of more than one purpose depending on the free will choices made during their life experience?

The incarnated soul experiences many moments and paths, which are navigated to learn, love, and experience the dynamics of physical life. Choices may open new pathways during a lifetime, providing an incarnated soul with many opportunities and paths, depending on decisions made by asserting free will.

These ideas feel logical to me given all the between-life regressions that bring up the notion of life planning and talk about souls actively studying life experiences while between physical lifetimes. However, it is unclear if there is one broad purpose or many smaller, more focused purposes.

The logic I use to ponder this question comes from my intuition and personal regression experiences. My thinking is as follows: if everything in life is predestined, there would be no need to study or plan during the time between incarnations. Why would souls need to study?

It is exciting to stay open to the possibility that the future will be full of interesting learning opportunities.

Personal rule #1: Stay open, trust your gut, and believe in the possibility of new things to come.

These are words I repeat to myself when I feel off balance or encounter life-changing moments, events, and scenarios. Think of all the incredible opportunities and experiences waiting for you. But we must remain open to the possibility.

Again, I am not a medical or psychology expert. I am just an inventor who has lived an incredible life. I like to think about big life-challenging moments in our lives as opportunities to reinvent our self.

Recap

How do I find a starting place to discover purpose? Join community groups, church groups, or clubs. Go on outdoor hikes with groups. Join social groups. Take a class.

Grab a friend and go to a painting class. Write. Exercise. Sing. Paint. Play music. Take up a hobby. Become a volunteer.

Interestingly enough, I thought I was too old to learn to play the guitar. But I realized no one is ever too old to start something new. I stay in the moment and enjoy the learning process. After six months of playing and practicing the guitar, I am enjoying the experience and taking lessons from a talented guitar teacher from across the country by way of the Internet and Skype.

Technology and opportunity have never been so abundant and readily available to assist us in discovering new things and finding activities that excite us. There are many resources available if you look for them.

Personal Rule #2: Stay true to yourself. Empower yourself. Love yourself.

Emotions

Major life situations are usually very emotional. As I have experienced these moments, I found it essential to seek out professionals, family, and friends to share my emotions. It is difficult for some of us to discuss feelings with another person, but it is important to try to do so.

Remember, your emotions may be closing you off to intuition or subtle whispers from beyond yourself. Messages and support can come from any place. The key is to do your best to stay open and let messages come to you. Trust messages will come from those who love you as well as from unexpected people and places.

Career Events

Career stress can also make for difficult times in our lives. Stress can kill. Every doctor tells us this is true. Many statistics highlight the negative health effects of stress.

When we decide our present career is too stressful or does not feel right, perhaps it is the right time for a change? After all, most of us spend a significant portion of our lifetime focused on our jobs and earning money to make ends meet. Staying in a situation that is not aligned with purpose is not healthy.

From my personal experience, the bottom line is if the job you are working at is causing significant stress, it is time to reevaluate what you are doing.

If you are dealing with a layoff or a situation where your job has been eliminated, and you loved that job, try to look forward. Job changes are difficult. Take a moment, breathe, and then think big picture. You know what you like to do, so focus on searching for a job doing work similar to the one you lost. It may even be in a different field.

Consider seeking out a professional counselor if you don't have friends or relatives available to talk with you. Remember you always have options even if you cannot see the possibilities in a particular moment.

Take some time to put together a plan, take classes to learn something new, and visualize what you want to do. If this is too difficult, just start by making a list of all your challenges. Prioritize your challenges, then start at number one and work down the list. Deal with each problem, one at a time.

Purpose

What excites you? What gets your attention? What makes you look up when you hear someone talking about it?

Sometimes all we need to do is pay attention. Take some time to think about these sort of questions. It may be an opportunity to access the Divine Library and soul records.

Frame the issues you want to ask. Say a little prayer for guidance or meditate on it. Then ask the question as explicitly as you can. As discussed, answers may not come quickly.

After sending your questions off, stay open to receiving responses. Answers may occur in a variety of forms from a clear thought suddenly popping into your head, a gut feeling, hearing a song over and over, having a friend say something that resonates with you, or learning something new.

Answers will come to you.

If you still feel stuck with no sign of a response, move out of your comfort zone. Take a trip. Take a class. Join a group. Change up your routine in healthy ways and be open to talking with people you do not know. It is your choice. Lovingly assert your free will to find the happiness you seek.

Last but not least, trust it to be true that you are here for a reason.

Chapter 13
Putting Lessons into Motion: Divine Library Examples

This chapter applies the presented approach explored in this book to access the Divine Library. The process involves crafting a difficult question, sending it off to my Spirit Guides, and waiting to discover what comes back.

My inquiry: *Show me insights we souls need to know to better understand spiritual realms so that we may be inspired to get the most out of our life experience.*

The question is a broad one. It also implies the question, why are there different religions and spiritual beliefs? The spiritual elephant metaphor works for me to describe different spiritual perspectives, but I wondered if there is a better, more understandable approach to help readers understand spiritual realms?

What could an inventor discover or articulate that might help life become a little brighter and less painful for people like me who ask big questions and seek deeper understanding about existence and spiritual realms?

I sat still and meditated for a time—clearing my mind. When I felt relaxed with minimal noise and distraction, I sent out the inquiry with an informal prayer starting with a thank-you prayer for the blessings in my life. Then I framed why I was seeking answers and why the questions are important to me.

I used a very informal prayer process much like I am talking to a dear loved one. For me, simple works best. This may not be the best way for others as some readers may wish to recite a specific prayer each time. As discussed in earlier chapters, choose the process that works best for you.

The following is the response that came to me. Not in the

form of words or voices in my head. Instead, the answer came by way of thoughts, images, and emotions that I wrote down. The unexpected insights arrived as I was writing an e-mail to a friend. As I wrote the e-mail, I recognized what I had written to be more than the original subject of my e-mail. But I did not stop. I let the images and thoughts flow and continued to write.

Below is the result of that process in its unedited form. Read the following as information flow. I interpreted the incoming thoughts as I wrote them down.

Also, note I have included the bracketed text below. Within the brackets, I inserted comments sometime later to explain my interpretation and provide more background and reference sources.

I believe that the words flowed to me as insights from the Divine Library with help as needed from my Spirit Guides or other spiritual entities.

Example 1

Inquiry: *Show me insights we souls need to know to better understand spiritual realms so that we may be inspired to get the most out of our life experience.*

Response: *Think of using a chladni plate with sand on it and play around with different frequencies. The sand takes shape into interesting patterns depending on the frequency used.*

[Note regarding a Chladni plate: The German scientist Ernst Chladni experimented with acoustics. He researched different types of vibrations, which became the foundation for the scientific perspective of sound in the nineteenth century. "One of Chladni's inventions was a technique to study the motions of vibrating plates . . . 'Chladni's Plates,' as they came to be called, provided an early way to visualize the effects of vibrations on mechanical surfaces" (Smithsonian, n.d.).]

Applied to the universe, it is well known the underlying source is vibration. We also know each of us gives off our own unique vibration. Vibrations manifest by way of energy flow while we are incarnate.

Now extrapolate and imagine each person to be a chladni plate. Each person is vibrating and our vibrations are interacting to form new vibrations. As humans have evolved and lived life over the millennia, these vibrations manifest into the human created world.

This includes religious beliefs, other spiritual thinking, traditions, economics, societies, and so on. As the veil is pulled back, humankind's limitation is obvious and fundamental.

Simply put, human languages and means of communication have shaped our view of the physical universe. This is obvious in many ways such as different religions and spiritual beliefs around the world often described as the divide between Eastern and Western ways of thinking and believing. It is not a surprise.

But dig further. Many believe we create our own universe and as such our own life experience. Again, this is just a two-dimensional view of higher dimensions. There is truth in it, but it is only two-dimensional truth. That is, it is one slice or view of reality. There are many other views. They are all points of truth on an infinite line.

As this is explored further, it becomes clear that language has shaped humankind's thinking. We have adjusted our vibrations to shape not only our view of the universe around us, but also our very existence as human beings.

You wonder what it all means when the experiences of NDErs around the world and regression experiences are considered? It means language has become such a part of the human life experience that it shapes even the images in one's mind and how people think.

Language is at the core of human communication, a description of reality, and manifests into physical form in the human world and continues to shape our collective vibration.

[Other thoughts came to me as I sat still while remaining open to what I was receiving.]

It seems there are many examples. Take the whale and its song, the birds and their song, and any other creatures on Earth that are relatively distant and apart from human vibration. The ant moves along happily doing what ants do. Each living thing on Earth has its own vibration and perspective of the physical world.

It should now be obvious that our reality and the reality that we visualize in our mind is not all of reality. It is manifested reality. In fact, it is even more fundamental. We are three- dimensional creatures with a worldview that is only two dimensional.

[Note that since we have three-dimensional experiences, I felt our worldview must also be three dimensional. I wanted to disagree with the thought, but I let the information continue to flow to try and understand it.]

As we bring other means of connecting into our worldview, only then can we begin to comprehend in three dimensions. Means of connecting includes prayer, meditation, abstract thought, creativity, love, compassion, empathy, other emotions, etc.

Our incarnate vibration can be shaped into anything we wish it to be. It can manifest. This comes by way of prayer, meditation, focused intention, etc. When one focuses so intensely with no constraints, dogma, or preconceived notions, one's vibration can cause ripples with other vibrations and result in strange things happening.

That's not to say humans have untapped super powers, but it is to say that in order to understand the true nature of self and how we perceive, interact, and exist, one must consider that shaping the view of heaven with two-dimensional thinking limits one's perspective.

It is hard to argue away the notion of self because I can look in the mirror and see myself. It is harder to understand that self can somehow control its own vibration and adjust the dial of frequency because when I look into that same mirror I cannot see such things.

Where does this leave us? I suppose these insights help us visualize spirituality represented by visions previously shared, an infinite pool where each drop in the infinite pool is only one way of thinking about spirituality.

[Note that the above paragraph related to a vision I had experienced during one of my earlier regressions discussed in book one. I understood the image I had experienced while under deep hypnosis to mean there are many perspectives about spirituality and the nature of existence. And yet, I still wondered about the reference to that vision showing up during this inflow of information. It was a bit jarring, but confirmed the ideas to be consistent with previous thoughts I had experienced.]

Using existing two-dimensional language to provide example and analogy is the only way to convey such insights to others. Writing comes to life as souls consume books, resulting in understanding, but with the side effect of manifestation.

[This idea of writings coming to life came to me during a regression. During that regression, I saw a book moving into the world. Then the book transformed into a bird and flew out of sight. It was really strange at the time, but I understand the visual to mean words come to life and transform as readers consume them.]

While it seems we are limited by way of language, knowing this limitation allows us to remove the veil and extrapolate, explore, and attempt to use the limitation of language to manifest new vibrations that can make one's life experience richer, more educational, and less painful.

[End of inflow.]

I understand most of the meaning of the information above, but I am still thinking about some of it. My first impression of this stream of thought was that my creative mind was engaged and just running off a bit.

But the more I thought about what I had written, the more I realized there was a deeper meaning behind it all. Even the style of writing was somewhat different in places.

Here is an image that came to me with the information I received:

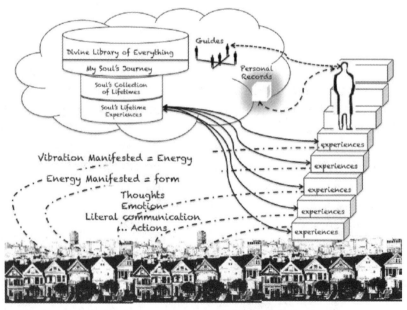

After a great deal of soul-searching and thinking about the information I had received, the above figure makes sense to me. The figure illustrates the relationship of language to our life experience. Language has affected our ability not only to communicate but also to comprehend complex and abstract concepts. Could this idea also relate to the notion that reality is an illusion? Have we shaped our reality by the way we communicate?

The language we use to describe our world is two dimensional when written on the page. Words have meaning, pushing language into the three-dimensional realm with the help of our brains. I think the conversion from words to meaning is where we tend to get ourselves into trouble given what we say and write can be interpreted differently.

Try communicating without words as an experiment. Look at a pet and try to tell someone what your pet is without using words. Or look at yourself in the mirror and imagine describing yourself to someone who does not know you. Can you pick the exact words that will help someone truly know you?

I know the experiment sounds ridiculous or obvious. But without words, we cannot communicate with each other in the earthly humanity-based environment we have built during our many lifetimes on this planet.

How do other life forms on our planet communicate?

Birds and whales sing, dogs bark, cats purr, low-frequency elephant calls travel through the ground, treehopper insects vibrating stems, kangaroo rats foot-drum communication, jumping spider vibrations, and so on.

It seems every species that I can think of, and I am no biologist, uses some other form of vibration or physical ability such as releasing pheromones to communicate. From my quick assessment, it seems more complex vibrations like music and song come with emotional context.

Ancient glyph, pictographs, petroglyphs, and logographic languages may have included emotional context too, but our present-day languages have limited emotional context—word choice is essential. Our means of communication consists primarily of only words, syntax, and semantics.

While reviewing an earlier draft of this book, Angela Thompson Smith commented, "This is why Ideograms in remote viewing are so powerful. A single glyph can contain all of the information contained in a picture, photograph, event, or video. Words are powerful but limited. Symbolic language is so much more powerful. I also believe that symbols also enter our consciousness more quickly: think road signs."

Don't get me wrong. Language has helped human beings progress in amazing ways, but one could argue word choice does not consistently convey intended emotion. Even words that are intended to refer to specific emotions may not describe one's feeling accurately. We often rely on the subtle aspects of communication such as body language and inflection.

In the 1953 book *Philosophical Investigations* by Ludwig Wittgenstein, which is recognized as one of the most important works in the field of philosophy in the twentieth century, he wrote: "If language is to be a means of communication there must be agreement not only in definitions but also . . . in judgments" (Wittgenstein 1953).

Wittgenstein pointed out that words provide names of objects where such meaning of the word must be taught. An issue arises when a word fixes meaning to an object since a relationship can only exist after defining language, context, and usage. "Talking about 'the meaning of a word' misleads us into thinking that there are fixed boundaries and strict definitions that determine our use of a word. If we examine how words are used, we will see this is not the case" (SparkNotes, n.d.).

I believe present-day languages confine our thinking to the structure created by it. We seem to miscommunicate more often than communicate. If we communicate in person, we can touch and use inflection. But sometimes it is still difficult to grasp the emotion behind spoken words. Great authors can accomplish this in their books. However, most of us do not have such talent.

If we do not understand the exact intended meaning of a word, we tend to become confused or misinformed then build other understanding on top of it. Continue with this line of thinking and expand it to topics that are difficult to comprehend.

Suddenly it becomes obvious that beliefs we cannot see or touch, such as higher dimensions, spirituality, and emotions, become extremely difficult to communicate and fully comprehend. The last part of the above response gave me clues for dealing with language limitations.

Changing languages to include emotional context by incorporating features such as song, art, photography, and imagery is unrealistic. But we can think beyond words and use analogy or metaphor to communicate spiritual concepts. We can also use illustrations and descriptions like I have used in this book to share our ideas.

Another solution is to avoid taking word meaning so literally that the words become the only truth while losing emotional context or grander notions of the intended communication.

I know this is a head-scratcher indeed. But as an inventor, I always start by working hard to define the problem to be solved then visualize many solutions and extrapolate solutions to determine if a particular solution will solve the defined problem.

As an inventor, when I visualize and validate in my mind that the solution will solve the problem, I can then bring the solution into reality with word specificity and diagrams. Essentially, I describe the solution well enough to build it and explain how it solves the original problem. Writing frames the problem to be solved and then transforms ideas into physical solutions that address the issue. As such, words and diagrams become products, systems, or processes.

Reflecting on how I work to comprehend higher dimensions, I also remind myself to remain open and avoid becoming bound by preconceived notions and present ways of thinking and interpretation.

This approach gives me the freedom to shape my thoughts into analogy and words. Sometimes it has allowed me to stack different spiritual ideas together to present new perspectives. The process enabled me to craft this book, and will be used to craft other works like it in the future. I enjoy the discovery process of researching higher dimensions from numerous first-hand experiences using language, analogy, and diagrams. It enables me to better understand complex spiritual topics.

As we collectively contemplate the limitation of language and remain open to the possibility of spectacular wonders we cannot see, hear, or touch, maybe the use of diagrams and analogy will aid in visualization and understanding. The process helps me appreciate the wonder and beauty of dimensions beyond this physical perspective.

Example 2

With the success of the last attempt to receive information from the Divine Library, I decided to try it again with a new inquiry. This time my question would be more complicated.

My reason for asking the following questions is from a desire to understand the mechanism behind connecting with each other and connecting beyond our self to spiritual realms.

Many of us contemplate "connecting" in the spiritual sense. So I wondered if this notion of connection is related to tuning into someone's vibrations like a ham radio operator might do to receive a radio signal, or if there is something else going on. I shaped my new inquiry and found it required multiple questions to clarify my investigation and intention.

New query: *How does the soul-to-soul connection process work while souls are incarnate? How does the connection process to the Divine Library work? Is the connection simply a tuning process or something different?*

The unedited response below came to me while shopping at a grocery store. I hurried home to write down what I had received. Note that I later included brackets to provide clarification, thoughts, and other ideas similar to the approach I used for my first inquiry.

Response: *Rather than looking at remote connection as tuning or channeling, one could think of it much like NDErs do when they are out of their body. Just by thinking about someone while in that state facilitates a visit with the person in their thoughts. This could be nearby or across the country or on the other side of the world. Consciousness has truly left the body in this case and the NDEr is experiencing an OBE.*

Compare this with a remote viewer who is attempting to connect with a target using a well-defined protocol so a target can be identified. The remote viewer is actually projecting their consciousness to the target and as such is able to describe it. In this way, consciousness has been projected through higher dimensions to a distant location or place.

Also compare remote viewing with receiving information from the Akashic Records or Divine Library. Consciousness is projected into higher dimensions and the library, enabling a person to connect to specific information on a particular topic, past life, or other area of interest.

Now expand all of this thinking. Think of every example of connecting as projecting one's consciousness into spiritual realms or higher dimensions. Consciousness can travel to higher dimensions and in doing so is able to view/access/experience connecting with other consciousnesses, including the Akashic Records or Divine Library.

[Side note: There is a phenomenon known as a shared death experience, which is another example of consciousness projection and consciousness outside of a physical body. "Peter Fenwick, MD, and Elizabeth Fenwick, RN, who research end-of-life phenomena, have collected hundreds of Shared Death Experiences in the United Kingdom and in Northern Europe. Dr. Raymond Moody formally coined the term 'Shared Death Experience' in his 2009 book, Glimpses of Eternity" (Shared Crossing Project 2017).

In Dr. Raymond Moody's book Glimpses of Eternity he writes of shared death experiences and suggests the existence of a heavenly plane, "This phenomenon, known as non- local memory, involves personal information that resides outside of an individual's brain" (Moody 2010, 38).]

There can also be a time component to such connections, if desired. Some remote viewers have applied their protocols to predict future outcomes.

[Side note: There are examples of predicting future outcomes using remote viewing. Author and retired US Army major Paul H. Smith, PhD, discusses what is known as associate remote viewing (ARV) in his book, The Essential Guide to Remote Viewing. Smith says asking a remote viewer to predict the outcome of a future event "would amount to little better than a guess. This is because the viewer's conscious mind ('left brain hemisphere') will weigh in, and despite the viewer's best efforts will begin speculating as to what the correct answer might be" (Smith 2015, 93). In other words, using the terminology as defined within this book, the remote viewer's Ego will likely interfere, making predictions unreliable. Smith goes on to say the issue is being addressed by remote viewing pioneers who have developed various ARV strategies that they believe increases the likelihood of prediction success.]

The key aspect of the remote viewing protocol is viewing the thing with which one wishes to see in the future, e.g. lottery numbers. By projecting one's consciousness into the next higher dimension, time works differently. Time is not linear thereby enabling a person who has projected their consciousness to see possible future events.

[It is worth considering the implication of cause and effect on the probability of specific event outcomes. It may be impossible to predict an outcome where more than one result could occur due to the free will assertion of crucial participants and its impact on potential effects as previously discussed in book one and chapter 7 of this book.]

Now for the rub: not all future events are certain. However, sometimes it is useful to see future possibilities to make course corrections to prevent an event that might happen given extrapolation of current events. Therefore, there are gatekeepers so to say—divine beings responsible for allowing consciousness travel and allowing access.

This ties back to the prayer many use to access the Akashic Records. The prayer is a focus of intention to ask for permission and clarify the reason for the requested information. If the consciousness of the Divine Library is willing, connection is made and information transfer occurs.

Therefore rather than tuning ones frequency into another consciousness, one projects their consciousness to connect with another willing consciousness. Willingness is key. One cannot simply force such a connection to occur.

What seems to be confusing is simply higher dimensional functionality viewed from lower dimensions. Details matter. To say tuning to another incarnated soul's vibration frequency to connect

is not correct. Rather, one projects their consciousness into higher dimensional realms to connect to other consciousnesses, creating a divine dance of ebbs and flows, reactions and interactions, love and emotion.
[End of information flow.]

I had received a great deal of information in what felt like a burst, and I did my best to recall what had come to me upon returning home. It would have been more efficient to have had a voice recorder or a pencil and paper handy. But trying to capture the information while in a public place like the grocery store with a cart full of groceries would have been challenging to say the least.

There had been a time delay from what I felt to be a data download to when I was able to document it. I tried not to embellish the information. However, I have noticed some embellishment during the process. I suspect the embellishment is a way to personally interpret and comprehend in-coming images, concepts, and thoughts. To avoid complicating what one receives and embellishing the information with opinion, I recommend writing it down as soon as it comes to you—the sooner the better.

The fundamental idea did feel like an ah-ha moment since I had previously assumed there to be a basic vibration tuning process going on for a connection to take place similar to the previous tuning fork example.

The insight related to a much more elegant and sophisticated process like a dance between two or more consciousnesses. I visualize this process as being similar to a stream of water with its ebbs and flows, mixing at times into an eddy where the water swirls. This swirling of water and mixing of vibrations is what I visualized as the "connection."

I tried to sketch a diagram to illustrate the idea of projecting one's consciousness but could not come up with a meaningful way to do so. A video animation may have worked but does not lend itself to a description in a book.

With this new idea in mind combined with my new perspective about how language affects our physical existence, I thought about this notion of projecting consciousness. Perhaps the way to project one's consciousness is to enter into a meditative state where our active mind, or ego, has been calmed, and then to visualize where one's consciousness will go. Once you feel a connection, visualize a mixing process. Swirling. Embracing. Sharing. Proceed to send and receive communication. Form thoughts to send. Receive thoughts. Ask for heavenly support for information and accept it. Experiment with the process and record your results.

From the work of remote viewers, it appears the use of precise protocols to establish a connection with a target then record incoming impressions about the target is a reasonable approach to facilitate a similar process with the Divine Library.

Meditation, focused intent, and deep hypnosis are other ways to establish a mind calming state. Apply the process of your choosing to enter such a state. Use visualization to project your consciousness. Lastly, enter a divine consciousness dance with the desired consciousness and connect.

I believe it is the visualization of where we wish to connect after our ego has been calmed that enables consciousness projection, connection, and communication.

Example 3

A new query: *How do we distinguish heavenly inspiration from our own thoughts/feelings?*

[At first, I received nothing. I thought this would be an easy one, but nothing. I just went about my day. Then an answer came to me in a one-word burst. It felt as if it had been shouted or strongly communicated to me. Not sure there is a word for exactly how it felt to receive the communication. It was not scolding or lecturing. It felt important to listen.]

Response: *PRACTICE.*

[I expected much more than this simple one-word answer. I get the simplicity of it, but I wanted to know more details. I asked another question: how do I practice such that answers become clear and untainted by my ego, i.e., my wants and desires.]

Think of it like this . . . when you play your guitar, do you feel you naturally know how to play it or do you feel you need to repeat the song you are trying to play until it just flows? You practice, of course.

Try different approaches. Work on remote viewing and feeling targets—do it for fun—do it to get used to feeling the subtleties of your intuition and our guidance. Play with dowsing and let energy flow into you—watch as subtle muscle movements answer questions you pose. Are you forcing this to happen or is it simply happening? The best way to tell the difference is by trial and error. The more you practice, the more you will learn what feels like intuition from heavenly sources **or** *what is actually your own ego reacting to the physical world around you. Pay attention to the responses you receive. Sometimes responses will come fast. Sometimes responses may take time. If you have a thought pop into your head, ask yourself does it feel like an answer or does it feel like a desired answer and thus your ego is in control?*

[I asked another question . . . Why is this so difficult?]

It is not difficult, as you say. It is a natural process, which has become unnatural for incarnated human souls. So just make it natural again through day-to-day practice and experimentation. Trust it. Try dowsing. Do it for fun and embrace the feeling. Let go of your earthly existence and allow us in all the time, not just when you feel you need us. But do not forget why you are alive. You are alive to experience life. If you knew all the right decisions or how to make life easy by winning the lottery, the lessons you wish to learn would become more difficult. Your challenges would be bigger. They would cause you more suffering and more lost lifetimes trying to learn the lessons you desired before your present incarnation.

[Angela Thompson Smith says, "Dowsing is simply allowing the body to be used as a tool to access information that is downloading into the subconscious mind: using tools such as a pendulum or L-rods, or a hand or finger scanning an Ideogram or map or time line."]

So open your heart and mind. Let the energy flow into you all the time. Then the big questions for which you seek answers will not seem so big. They will just be questions you answer like you do for all questions—with you heart, your intuition, and love. Play your incoming heavenly intuition like you play your guitar—free from ego.

> *Now get to work and practice.*

[End of inflow.]

This response felt bolder than others I had experienced. It felt urgent.

I had always wondered about channeling but believed my connection was more a shared connection rather than channeling as Cayce had experienced.

To be honest, the following shook me a bit: *"allow us in all the time, not just when you feel you need us."*

Interesting. The engineer part of me wanted to believe that I must have simply written down what I had expected to write down or made a typo of sorts. However, I have been very consistent about writing information coming to me with no editing, except for obvious typos.

I leave it to you to decide if the information I received was genuinely channeling or just my imagination embellishing the thoughts that came to me. The process did rock me a bit. I seriously considered editing parts of it out of this manuscript. But I decided it was vital for me to remain consistent. The entire information flow needed to stay in this book as received.

Summary

All of the concepts I received in responses, such as dowsing, will require further study. The topics may be worthy of more exploration. It is important to note that I do not think of the response I received in these examples as the only possible answers to my questions. But these answers resonated with me. I felt truth in them.

In an upcoming chapter, it will be your turn to try out the process by asking personal questions. But before I ask you to do that, the next chapter will shape some of the received insights into ideas about the evolution of communication. I will also present ideas about problem solving in a group of like-minded individuals.

Chapter 14
Evolving Communication: Example Ideas

After receiving insights in previous chapters, I wondered what I might do to enhance earthly languages and apply the previously presented ideas to project one's consciousness. Can we reinvent ourselves and in doing so evolve the way we communicate with each other?

Reflecting on my approach to writing this book, I applied concepts typically used for building systems in our 3D world to deduce understanding of perceived systems and processes in higher dimensions.

Evolving Communications

If we assume that we are more than what we can see, touch, and hear, then we can imagine ourselves as more than the physical creature we see in the mirror. As I have learned, it is important to remember that the purpose of our life experience is to learn and grow.

Sitting on top of a mountain feeling energy may be fine for a time; but at some point, one must get back into the dynamics of physical life and experience all of it—get back into the game.

With a new awareness of spiritual realms, I am confident we can find a way to live a connected life and experience joy while evolving the methods used to communicate beyond the vibrations shaped into spoken words with implied meaning.

That said, great authors write books full of beautiful words. I am suggesting we consider embracing the notion that words on the page require conversion into understanding and personal meaning.

When the subject of our communication is spiritual, we still read or hear words and translate them into meaning. I remind myself that the words used to describe spirituality represent only a slice of higher dimensions.

What if we treated ourselves as a multidimensional translator? All that is required is reading or listening beyond the words we hear or read then converting those words with our minds into meaning. For example, putting aside the notion of a consciousness connection for this discussion, let us explore what happens when people are communicating.

We know people send out vibration during communication. Our ears detect the audio waves. We convert vibrations into words and translate the words with our brains to manifest understanding.

In an attempt to solve the challenge of emotion and word meaning, ideograms such as emojis have attempted to offer context and emotion for blogs, website posts, text messages, instant messages, and e-mail messages.

When communicating in person, we project emotion by way of voice inflection, body language, speech intensity, pitch, and volume. Communication can become animated when we are emotional. Suddenly, we find ourselves speaking words driven by feelings in the moment. Sometimes we verbalize impulsive thoughts we do not mean.

From the perspective of the listener, we often do not fully understand the emotion coming at us by only the words we hear. We also listen to the volume and passion in a person's voice as they speak to us. We combine all these elements during communication into assumed meaning.

Occasionally we get defensive; shouting and passion prompt animated arguments. We make assumptions about the emotion coming at us and protect ourselves. An immediate impression is formed in our minds from our perspective.

If we can find a way to stay open and call on our intuition during an emotional conversation, we might be able to understand the true meaning of what is being communicated and recognize the reason behind the emotion.

In some cases, there may be an excellent reason to engage our defenses to protect ourselves. In other cases, we might be able to deal with the situation with love and understanding by adjusting our defensive reactions.

What if we visualized that we are multidimensional sensors with the ability to process vibrations, emotions, and feelings? What if we connected to the energy coming at us and tried to calm it? What if we visualized wrapping a comforting blanket around the person who is shouting? "Just imagine."

Granted, this sounds like a beautiful utopia without consideration for the reality of life and dynamic interactions with people. If you feel safe in a given situation, try it with loved ones to see if it works for you. Take a moment to listen beyond the words. Try to understand what is being communicated on a deeper level.

By listening to the words, feeling the emotion, and remaining open, I think we may be able to understand before reacting then respond with loving words and energy.

I know where I have had difficulties communicating with other people. It has typically been when I overreacted, made assumptions, or responded too quickly. I did not try to connect with the vibrations being communicated to me. I heard only words and allowed my emotions into the translation process.

I recommend we build our virtual version of an internal communication translator and activate it when we communicate. It is crucial to remember that two people may hear the same words, but interpret the words differently.

I am simply suggesting we think more about communication and word choice. Consider the idea that words have limited our beliefs and narrowed the perspective of who we are and what we are capable of becoming.

I believe misinterpreted communication has limited our collective growth. If we embrace the notion that our beliefs are only impressions based on experience and personal interpretation, we might be able to open ourselves up to a vast number of new perspectives and embrace deeper meaning and understanding.

Communication coming to us is a combination of audio vibrations and other higher vibrations undetectable by our eyes and ears. When we apply these concepts to spiritual discussion and open up to the possibility of different ways of thinking and viewing spirituality, we can grow beyond the words that have limited our thinking.

I believe it is possible to see the world as vibration and energy by visualizing the energy people radiate. Then consume or absorb that energy and translate what you feel into meaning. Move beyond physical reactions and let your soul connect to the person communicating. What do you feel?

I hope someday this will be the new way we communicate.

To kick-off the expansion of personal communication, all we need to do is remember that words are limiting. Move beyond the two-dimensional "words on a page" view of our three- dimensional world and open up to a world full of wonder, enhancing life experience without threatening our individual beliefs.

An open mind can make relationships more profound and more rewarding. It allows us to connect with the world and other people in our unique way. Have fun with it. Take some time and truly listen to the physical world then reach beyond it.

Imagine sending a message off to the birds singing in your backyard. Imagine you are communicating with the bird. Then realize you are indeed interacting with the bird and the bird is trying to understand. This sort of communication does not mean you have superpowers. You are just connecting with the world in a natural, fun, and new way.

Use the figure below and your imagination to build your version of a translator. Put the translator into action. Switch it on. What do you feel?

You can remain grounded in the physical world while embracing the vibrations you are receiving, and then sending out your vibrations in the form of communication.

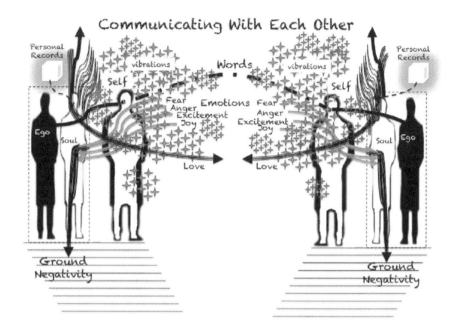

From my experience using this sort of visualization, the physical world becomes brighter and more vivid. Do those words sound familiar?

If you study NDEs as I have done in my books, you will recall these words are typically used by NDErs to describe their experience. By working together to open up our minds, we can make this world brighter, more vivid, and more real than real.

Group Problem Solving

One approach to working on the more significant issues of the day is to work in a group to search for answers. Groups work together every day to solve problems at work or in family units related to all sorts of products, technologies, and issues. There are prayer groups and groups of people meditating with focused intention.

Using what we have discovered about the Divine Library,

let us apply these concepts to a group of incarnated souls similarly to how Newton, Cannon, De Tamble, and others talk about souls training together in soul groups.

The first step in the process is to form a group of like-minded individuals who agree on a particular problem to be solved. This process is similar to how companies brainstorm product development priorities or to solve product problems.

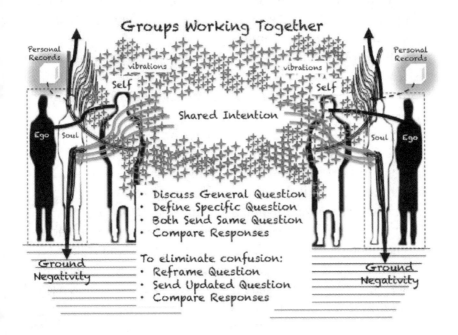

In this case, the group focuses initially on describing the problem of interest. Once there is an agreement regarding the issue, the group should work together to craft a question requesting a solution.

It is tempting to try to come up with immediate solutions. For many problems, such an approach is a great way to find a solution by brainstorming the problem and solving it based on what you already know.

But for those more significant problems, it makes sense to access the Divine Library to search for answers. Given the assumption that the Divine Library contains every vibration and energy fluctuation that has ever occurred, the information to solve the problem must be located somewhere in the library. All we need to do is shape our inquiry with specificity to visualize and be clear on our intention to receive specific information.

While working in a group, define the specific question each group member will focus on with loving intention. Then send it out as a group.

If we solve significant problems by accessing the Divine Library together in a group, we may receive new perspectives that can be collectively shaped into better solutions.

Send out the inquiry then take some reasonable amount of time to collect notes and thoughts that come. Ask each member of the group to write down their thoughts and ideas in a notebook. Draw sketches too.

Let's say the group agrees to get back together in a week. When you meet up, give all group members an opportunity to share the information in their notebooks. Note similar solutions, but don't disregard outliers until the group decides to do so.

After each group member is done sharing their work, have the group agree on the top three approaches. If a team member is passionate about one of the ideas, put it on your overall solution list.

Once the list has formed, put together an action plan as to how best to implement the plan. Grow group membership as needed to solve different problems.

This approach is very similar to brainstorming with one significant difference. The group is like-minded in that they all believe the Divine Library contains the answers that they can access.

It might help to have each group member focus on the question at a particular time of day regardless of location. Set a time for the group to send out the same inquiry. If answers are not coming, perhaps the question(s) must be refined or more specific. Be relentless and determined.

I believe answers will come to you.

Chapter 15
Putting Lessons into Motion: Example Exercises

In chapters 13 and 14, I presented examples regarding accessing and interpreting Divine Library information. This chapter provides sample questions for further exploration. I encourage you to modify these questions or form new questions then access the Divine Library for insights.

Note these questions are just examples. Both the questions and the insights you may receive will relate to your unique perspective, so interpret the responses you receive accordingly. Enhance your inquiries to the Divine Library with personal meaning. Ask the questions from your perspective.

Expect responses to arrive at unexpected times. Incorporate your existing understanding of spiritual realms with new ideas that come to you. Keep a notepad handy and sketch out the information and ideas by way of images, thoughts, and words.

There is no right or wrong approach to this process. There is only connecting and embracing your connection with spiritual realms.

Once you are comfortable with the method, practice by creating a new list of personal and general questions. Use the process to ask for insights. Write down what comes to you.

Remember some answers may not come to you quickly. Some responses may take longer than you desire. Just try to remain open-minded. From my experience, responses will eventually come.

Side note: The way I tell the difference between the heavenly answers I write and my wants and desires is by just asking myself the following question: Is this a thoughtful response or one that contains some form of fear, personal wishes, or personal desires?

Does the response reinforce the perspective causing me pain or does it offer a new one for me to think about?

Example Questions

Here are some examples to try or to modify into personal questions. Remember to trust your intuition and use your best judgment to take action or not. It is ultimately your decision to decide how to assert your free will to deal with the issues of interest.

Inquiry #1: *Regarding the notion about personally shaping reality—how can I modify my perspective of the world to make my life better?*

Inquiry #2: *How do I become more aligned with my life purpose?*

Inquiry #3: *How can I help other souls who ask me to help them become aligned with their life purpose?*

Inquiry #4: *What words of wisdom can I share with [insert name] who is struggling to remember their life purpose?*

Inquiry #5: *If time is an illusion, how can I leverage time to enhance my existing life experience.*

Inquiry #6: *The idea of growing while progressing through this life experience feels daunting in this moment. What can I do to make my experience more joyous?*

Personal Questions

Try writing additional questions in your notebook. Write questions that are personal and relate to your life. Details matter. Craft deeply personal and important questions that you feel are important.

Have fun with the process and try not to get frustrated.

If you are having difficulties, start by writing simple questions in your notebook.

Once you get the hang of the process, add complexity to your questions and more detail. I like to think about the saying from one of Aesop's fables, *The Tortoise and the Hare*, as a reminder to pace myself, "Slow and easy wins the race."

Review your initial questions and the responses you received from time to time to verify progress.

The more you practice, the easier the process will become.

Chapter 16
The Space between the Space

I often hear some people say we create our own reality, we are cocreators of this present life experience, and our thoughts manifest the universe we live in. I wonder how this is possible considering there are billions of other incarnated souls sharing this moment with me.

Are we all creating our own version of reality and our own universe? Are these people referring to personal perception or do some literally believe each one of us manifests our reality?

I wonder how can I create my own universe when I am sharing this moment in this physical space with billions of other incarnated souls and possibly countless other life forms throughout the universe.

To answer my questions, I explore them from two points of view: a big picture view and a more personalized point of view. Leading expert on out-of-body experiences and author of many books including Adventures in the Afterlife, William Buhlman (among others) refers to the big picture point of view as shared consciousness where incarnated souls share this present moment.

The following diagram illustrates my incarnated soul experience in this present moment. It also shows a cluster of souls directly sharing this moment with me. Additionally, other incarnated souls who indirectly share this moment with me are reflected in the clusters of clusters of souls part of the diagram.

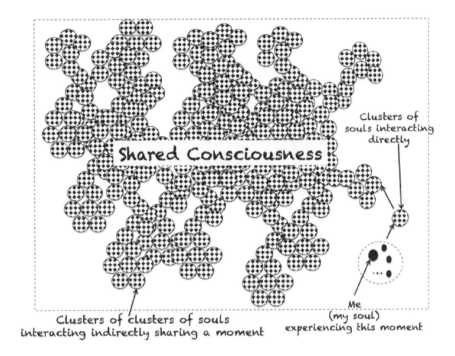

Clusters of souls interacting directly

Shared Consciousness

Me (my soul) experiencing this moment

Clusters of clusters of souls interacting indirectly sharing a moment

My specific point of view relates to my lifetime experience, as discussed in book one, where I experience daily life within a shared consciousness framework or soul school.

Living in a shared consciousness framework means the basic framework for my life experience includes the co-development of society, culture, economy, etc., with other incarnated souls who are experiencing this moment together. Such a framework allows each incarnated soul to experience and grow through both a personal experience within the framework of a shared consciousness experience and a shared consciousness experience by way of an infinite number of external cause-and-effect scenarios affecting, or being affected by, my personal life experience.

This idea of personal point of view combined with a shared consciousness point of view provides a grand perspective, but it still does not answer the question regarding the mechanism that enables my consciousness to interact beyond those incarnated souls with whom I interact.

How does my consciousness experience connectedness,

precognitions, paranormal scenarios, and astral travel (OBE) outside of a physical body? How am I able to receive unsolicited information or connect with a consciousness a billion light years away or in another dimension within the multiverse?

Maybe I can project my consciousness into higher dimensions or spiritual realms? But does projection even make sense given my consciousness exists across all dimensions simultaneously? Perhaps all I need to do is focus my intention and vibration within a given dimension on other consciousnesses sharing that dimension in order to share an experience with them?

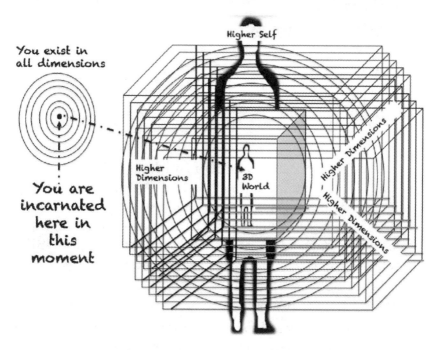

It also seems reasonable to assume a dimensional boundary or buffer exists between spatial dimensions to facilitate a soul's transition or vibration adjustment from one dimension to another.

Connecting

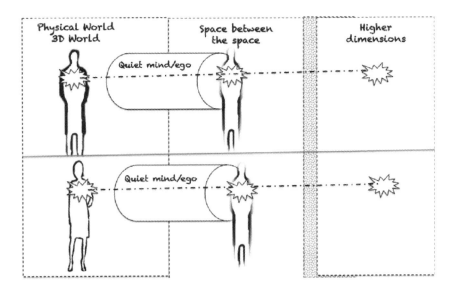

For example, such a transition may be how NDErs move from their physical body toward a light and how OBErs astral project. The process of transition would provide a staging mechanism for a soul to increase its vibration or re-phase and refocus intention before entering higher dimensions. Or in the case of some OBErs, this buffer realm may be where they intend to explore.

Near-Death Experiencers

Recall from book one some NDErs suddenly find themselves out of their physical body, attempting to communicate with people, but unable to do so. Many have reported hearing the conversations of people around them such as doctors, EMTs, and nurses. Others have walked through people, walls, and ceilings. After returning to their body, some NDErs have confirmed the conversions of the people around them, observed from above their body.

Out-of-Body Experiencers

Another group of experiencers are those who have an out-of-body experience (also known as astral projection) without having a near-death experience. Many believe OBErs are experiencing consciousness outside of a physical body and exploring spiritual realms.

After leaving their physical body, many OBErs report first exploring familiar environments such as their bedroom or house before moving on to exploring more distant locations.

Bob Monroe in his 1971 book, *Journeys out of the Body*, and William Buhlman's 1996 book, *Adventures beyond the Body*, have described their out-of-body experiences in their books where they use various techniques to leave their physical body, then travel to destinations by setting their intention.

For OBErs destination can range from familiar locations to other realms or what may be referred to as astral planes. I found it interesting that Monroe's and Buhlman's description of leaving the body appears to be very similar to NDEr reports of leaving their body during a near- death experience.

The *Space between the Space*

This buffer realm between the third (spatial) dimension and the fourth (spatial) dimension may be the realm experienced by both NDErs and OBErs. It seems reasonable to make the case for such a spiritual buffer realm. Further, it would be consistent to suggest this buffer realm to be where one's consciousness goes during a remote viewing experience, telepathy, connecting with spiritual entities such as guides or teachers, experiencing precognition, channeling, and other paranormal experiences.

This is not to say the spiritual journey of our consciousness is limited to such a buffer realm, but it seems logical to presume such a realm exists and supports paranormal experiences.

I call this buffer or spiritual realm the "*space between the space.*" I believe it exists between our physical 3D dimension and the next higher 4D dimension. Within this in-between realm an energetic reflection of the 3D world exists. This is where I believe our consciousness is able to interact with energetic reflections of the 3D world while out of body. In other words, our consciousness interacts with energy in the space between the space. It is through this mechanism of interacting with the energetic reflections of 3D physical things that allows incarnated souls to be cocreators in the 3D world of physicality and physical things.

Extrapolating on this notion of a *space between the space* I will further define it as the realm where my consciousness can travel while I am in a very relaxed or hypnogogic state, experiencing an NDE, or experiencing an OBE. Interacting in this realm enables me to experience a shared consciousness experience with other consciousnesses anywhere in the physical 3D universe.

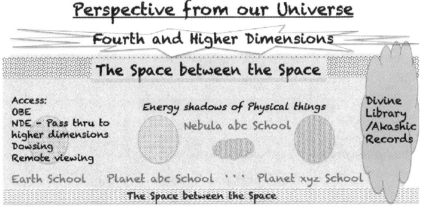

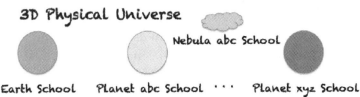

With the *space between the space* defined and adding in the concept that each of us is connected to all dimensions simultaneously, it seems reasonable to presume we incarnated souls are not physically going anywhere when we have such experiences. Rather, we are simply refocusing our intention or focus to other dimensions and in-between realms.

Thus, in the practical sense where experiencers experience dimensions beyond our three spatial dimensions by way of intention, NDE, OBE, or other experience shifts the point of view of my consciousness from the physical body to spiritual realms.

The purpose of the *space between the space* appears to be a gateway for one's subconscious, or consciousness, into higher dimensions. It is a transitory realm where one's consciousness is free from a physical body, and it enables connection with other consciousnesses in our three-dimensional physical universe where we can experience the energetic reflection of the 3D universe. It additionally enables one's consciousness to connect with spiritual entities and other entities in higher dimensions.

Higher Dimensions

The Space between the Space
Consciousness Play ground while incarnated

- Energy Shadows of physical things
- Dreams
- Lucid Dreams
- OBE
- Simulations
- Premonitions

- NDE transition place
- Intuition
- Connection with higher realms
- Past-life regression
- LBL regressions
- Accessing Divine Library
- Meditation

3D Physical Universe

Our Universe   Universe abc   · · ·   Universe xyz

The *space between the space* further enables incarnated souls to access information such as that from the Divine Library as described earlier and the same realm remote viewers and dowsers access to obtain information either directly by the remote viewer or indirectly by the dowser via involuntary micro-muscle movements powering pendulums, rods, or other physical devices.

There does not appear to be any limitation to consciousness connection possibilities. All it takes is focusing intention, setting the ego aside by way of meditation or other relaxation techniques, and directing one's subconscious.

FOCUS	TECHNIQUE/PROTOCOL
OBE - Astral Projection	Combination of body asleep, mind awake numerous techniques
Past-Life Regression	Guided hypnosis process with hypnotherapist or CD
NDE	External or health event
Between-life hypnotherapy	Guided hypnosis process and deepening techniques with hypnotherapist or CD
Meditation	Self-guided relaxation to shut down ego
Divine Library Access (Akashic Records)	Self-guided relaxation to shut down ego, automatic/spontaneous writing, channel, etc.
Dowsing/Remote Viewing	Relaxation, ego silencing, use micro-muscle movement, specific protocols
Channeling	Connection to external consciousness

Techniques for Accessing the Space between the Space

Focused intention appears to be the key for directing one's consciousness. For example, it requires intention to enable one's consciousness to take a particular action such as experiencing an OBE, communicating with one's spirit guide, psychically communicating with another consciousness, seeking information from the Divine Library, and so on.

In book one, hypnotherapy, guided self-hypnosis, and meditation were shown to be useful in setting aside the ego and focusing intention on objectives such as healing, learning about prior lives, learning about the time between lives, and other explorations.

Connecting

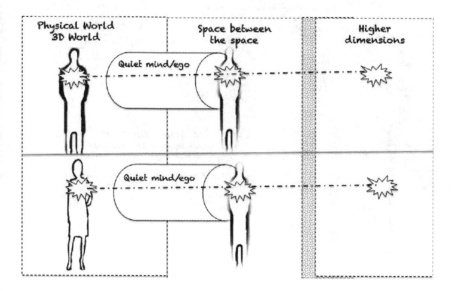

In earlier chapters, the Divine Library was accessed using techniques to connect to information for answering questions about our life experience and our soul's journey. This same process can be used for telepathy, communication, and other paranormal insights.

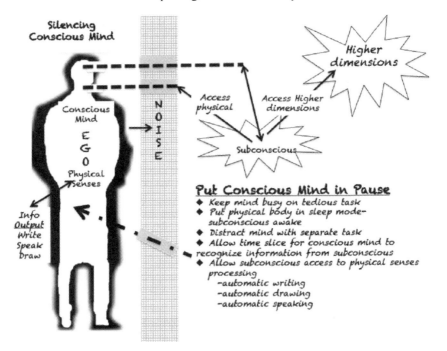

The approach I use is to have a conversation inside my head without speaking aloud. As presented in previous chapters, I usually start by being thankful for blessings in my life then go on to describe and explain the situation of interest using my inner voice. I follow up with a statement describing why I am requesting assistance.

After clarifying the situation and my intent, I use the following approach or protocol:

1. Trust the information I am seeking exists. I remain open-minded to the notion that my inquiry will be heard and the desired information is available.

2. Visualize the category of information where answers will be located. To receive information related to my inquiry, visualize the data is stored in the Divine Library and is available to me.

3. Quiet my mind. I apply the same techniques for self-hypnosis, prayer, or meditation to quite my Ego, and then I send out a loving prayer, meditate, and open up to receive guidance from heavenly realms.

4. Define exactly what knowledge or insights are desired; focus intently on receiving a response to my inquiry.

5. Take notes (without judgment or evaluation) in my notebook of what impressions come to me. As thoughts, feelings, and ideas arrive related to my inquiry, I document what comes to mind using words and sketches. I write it all down without editing or judgment.

6. After a time, I review the information I have written down and attempt to understand the content of information. I try to determine how the received insights relate to my inquiry.

Comparisons

Comparing the process I use to the techniques used by some OBErs for out-of-body experiences, all approaches share the common objective of quieting the conscious mind to allow the subconscious to journey inward without interference from one's ego, and by using focused intention as a guide to the desired experience.

FOCUS	Relaxed State	Quiet Mind Deeper than Relaxed	Mind Asleep Body Awake	Protocol Used	Technique Used
OBE			X		X
Past-Life Regression/ NDE	X	X			Guided
Between-life hypnotherapy Spontaneous OBE		X	X		Guided
Meditation, Prayer	X	X			Breathing Mantra Language
Divine Library Access (Akashic Records)	X	X		X	X
Dowsing	X	X			X
Remote Viewing	X	X		X	
Channeling		X	X		

Telepathy and Extraterrestrial Communication

Applying the concept that our consciousness works with energetic reflections within the space between the space realm, we can think of this realm as a gateway for our consciousness to access the unique vibrations of our 3D universe, or journey into higher dimensions as depicted in the following diagram.

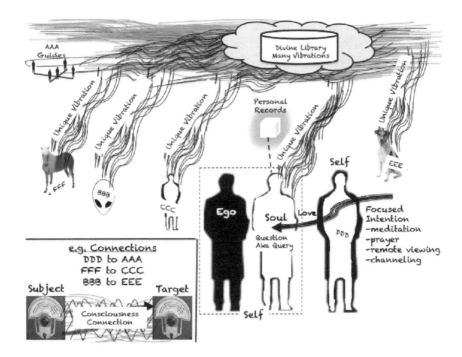

With my consciousness free from my physical body and focused by way of intention, I can further use the mechanism of the *space between the space* for telepathic communication between two or more consciousnesses. Expanding my awareness to include the existence of the space between the space assists my consciousness with connection to any other consciousness within the 3D universe, including extraterrestrials or any other conscious entity.

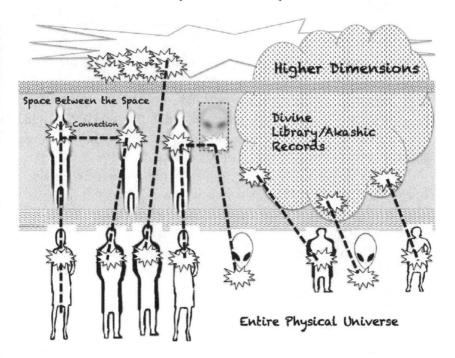

Telepathic Communications

Continuing to expand on the presented ideas, a mechanism for telepathic communication could then be considered an energetic connection between consciousnesses within the *space between the space.*

I find the telepathic process to be extremely subtle, requiring a tremendous amount of concentration, relaxation, and practice. This makes repeatability difficult at best and is often hit or miss.

American physicist, parapsychologist, and author, Russell Targ developed an ESP trainer in 1965 that he offers today as a free App, ESP Trainer, to provide immediate feedback for users to get in touch with the psychic part of themselves. Targ says he created the training device for people to figure out what it feels like so one can recognize a psychic experience. (*Richard Doland Show* 2019).

I have tried Targ's trainer and found it to be very interesting. As I worked with the App over time, I concentrated on how I felt when I made a selection. The more I practiced with it, the more I started to recognize being drawn to one selection over another.

The process felt similar to dowsing where an ideomotor

response (e.g., automatic micro- muscle movements) to a question affects the swing or rotation of a pendulum (weighted object such as a crystal that is hung from a single cord or small chain) at the end of a cord or small chain.

With dowsing, one concentrates on receiving answers to questions. Answers are said to prompt an ideomotor response of the dowser's hand, causing the pendulum to swing or rotate a certain way based on the users training of the device (Newcombe, n.d.).

Dowsing experts believe answers come from the dower's subconscious, resulting in micro-muscle movements of the dowser's hand, prompting the pendulum to rotate or swing a specific way to answer questions.

After building some confidence in my dowsing results, I decided I would try the same techniques of leveraging micro-muscle movement. However, with Targ's ESP Trainer App, I used my eyes and concentrated on relaxing then waited to "feel" my eyes gravitate to one possible answer. I presumed if I could relax, micro-muscle movements associated with my eyes would cause me to peer toward the correct colored box in Targ's App.

After a great deal of practice, I had some success with this approach. Once I felt my eyes move toward a particular colored box, I concentrated on that "feeling," as Targ suggests, in order to remember how it "felt."

While my practice did appear to increase my success rate, the process was not consistent. Honestly, in some ways successful selections felt similar to my experiences with intuition.

Most of us have experienced the subtle nature of intuition. It is difficult to trust at times. But when we do trust our intuition, we are often surprised and pleased with ourselves when the received intuition insights save our backside.

To increase the success rate of psychic experiences, protocols have been developed by experts in the areas of remote perception and dowsing. Given this success, I suggest the development of protocols for psychic communication may be worth exploring to increase the probability of success.

After numerous experiments, I found my success rate for accessing the Divine Library, remote viewing, and dowsing to be much higher than my success with telepathy. I suspect this is due to the dynamic nature of consciousness-to-consciousness connection compared to receiving fixed information or specific answers. As such, I decided to try to expand my protocol for receiving information from the Divine Library to include consciousness-to-consciousness communication.

With the unreliable success rates of historical telepathic approaches, I am hopeful the use of a protocol with an emphasis on the use of imagery and sensory information instead of language may garner some success and repeatability.

After experimentation and testing, I have come to the following conclusions: (1) a very relaxed or meditative state is required to have any kind of success, (2) it helps to imagine one's consciousness existing in an energetic realm, or what I call the *space between the space*, to connect and interact with the energetic reflection of an intended target, and (3) the use of images and other sensory information for communication rather than language (words) seems to enhance the experience.

The issue with trying to perceive language, or words, appears to be due to inconsistency of how people use language with respect to context and meaning. To work around such limitations, I send messages using mental images, short sequences of mental images, sounds, emotions, and other sensory information. I avoid using language.

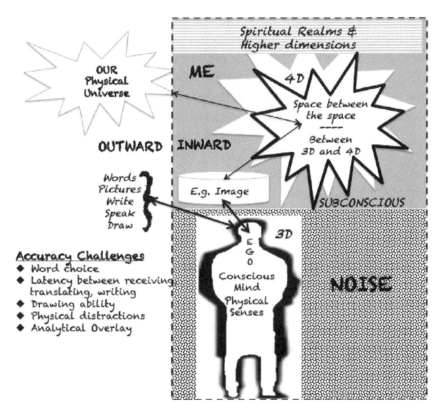

I wonder if a protocol for telepathy should include a process similar to that of establishing a connection like a computer when it communicates with another computer? Could such a connection enable information flow between communicating consciousnesses?

While I continue to have some success, more work is required. I have come to believe it takes a great deal of practice to "feel" the subtle nature of the subconscious information. But I remain hopeful more research, experimentation, and testing will prove telepathy to be a learned skill that anyone can master.

Telepathic Process or Protocol

The first step in my protocol for telepathy requires imagining the *space between the space* and an energetic reflection of the 3D universe. Then I establish a connection with an intended consciousness by sending out focused emotional thoughts such as concentrating on the person's name, an image of the person, or description of the person.

Once I feel a connection has been established, I send out imagery-based messages and receive imagery in a very relaxed or hypnagogic state with a specific intent or question in mind.

It is interesting to note that there is no distance limit or time orientation related to communication within the *space between the space*. So communication can occur with any consciousness in the multiverse in the past, present, or future.

I further assume there to be limitations. For example, both consciousnesses must share the intent, or question, and the desire to communicate. Additionally, images must contain shared meaning and context. And finally, a timeframe for such communication must be agreed upon and integrated within the intent of both communicating subjects. A timeframe may also be implied by the intent of wanting to communicate in this now moment.

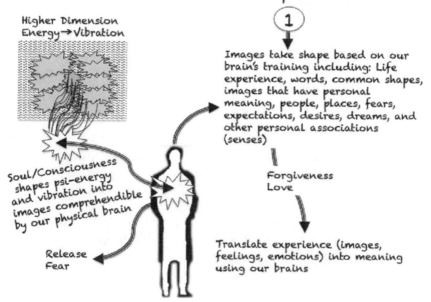

**Information from Higher Dimensions
Translation and Interpretation**

Higher Dimension
Energy → Vibration

(1)

Images take shape based on our brain's training including: Life experience, words, common shapes, images that have personal meaning, people, places, fears, expectations, desires, dreams, and other personal associations (senses)

Forgiveness
Love

Soul/Consciousness shapes psi-energy and vibration into images comprehendible by our physical brain

Release
Fear

Translate experience (images, feelings, emotions) into meaning using our brains

To receive information it is helpful to establish a narrow band of intent. If intent is not narrow, the conscious mind may add in information to the desired raw information, attempting to fill in gaps, find patterns, add personal meaning, and include additional unrelated information.

Thus, in order to receive raw information a systematic approach such as a protocol must be established to minimize unrelated information or noise.

Systematic approaches discussed earlier such as remote viewing, automatic writing, hypnosis, and entering trance states are methods for connecting to subconscious information, but the subtle nature of the information makes it difficult to differentiate relevant in-coming information from embellished ideas or information.

Belief in the existence of the information, learning how it feels to receive information, a great deal of practice, and successful attempts at receiving information will build confidence and sharpen our natural abilities.

Below is the prototype protocol for telepathic experimentation. Test it yourself to see if it will work for you or modify it as needed. Free will applies—in other words, both you and the target of your telepathic communication must want to communicate.

There may also be some way to use visualization to amplify the process, but this idea also requires experimentation and further testing.

A Protocol Prototype

- Focused intent: visualize the energy realm where communication will take place, visualize the intended target, visualize the timeframe such as now, and imagine a connection is establish.

- Focused telepathic probe or ping (love vibration [preferred] or other emotion). Send out this probe multiple times until subject responds back.

- Sender translates their message into a series of images or a video stream.

- Sends the images to their subject.

- For two-way communication, a response may be sent

by way of images back to the sender.

• While I do not believe a closing probe is required, it is generally a good idea for subjects to agree on something or some image that signifies the termination of the communication burst.

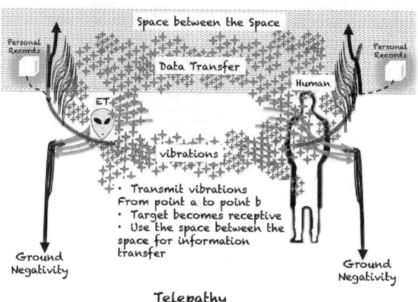

I think consistency also requires the right state of mind and mastery of imagery, feelings, and emotions. Try expanding your experiments with these ideas to connect with a remote consciousness, such as an ET, in some part of our galaxy or universe.

Establish your intent to receive in-coming responses with the caveat that you will not allow such ET communication to have a negative energy effect on you and you will not be open to any kind of nefarious intent from a sender.

Be open to listen to any responses you receive by way of feelings, emotions, images— write everything down. I have had some success with this process, but I am still experimenting and working on making a protocol for ET communication personally useable.

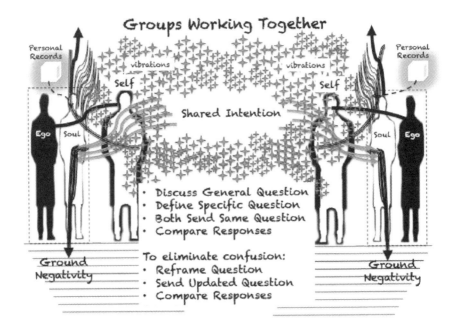

What about groups? Can we team up in groups to intensify telepathic communication?

I honestly believe our future communication will expand beyond language to include some form of telepathy as more and more people discover telepathic communication is possible by visualizing the energetic realm of the *space between the space* and a great deal of practice.

Chapter 17
Cocreative Consciousness

One of my most incredible moments of understanding occurred when I realized that I exist in all dimensions simultaneously. Visualizing a slice through other dimensions, I begin to understand how to create/shape my 3D reality. My consciousness is not merely my physical body. I understand that I am experiencing a unique life experience while simultaneously being connected to everything. My explorations of bi-location and consciousness have proven to me that I can expand my perception of "me" by visualizing both the physical and energetic aspects of me.

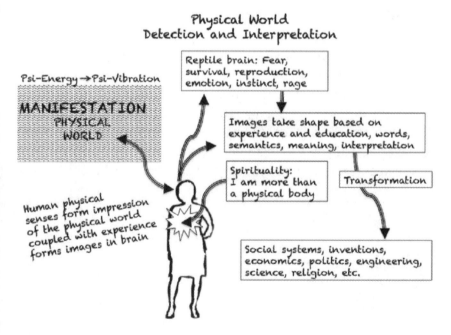

Physical World
Detection and Interpretation

Psi-Energy → Psi-Vibration

MANIFESTATION
PHYSICAL
WORLD

Reptile brain: Fear, survival, reproduction, emotion, instinct, rage

Images take shape based on experience and education, words, semantics, meaning, interpretation

Spirituality:
I am more than a physical body

Transformation

Human physical senses form impression of the physical world coupled with experience forms images in brain

Social systems, inventions, economics, politics, engineering, science, religion, etc.

As I visualize and expand my awareness into the energetic realm of the *space between the space*, my visualizations transform from thought to energy, ultimately manifesting in the physical world as physical, social, and economic creations.

Once I believe it is possible to expand my present experience to include the energetic aspect of me, I become a cocreator of my experience by way of the energetic part of me. I can even focus the energetic aspect of me to help me communicate with another person by visualizing my connecting with this other person's consciousness.

I visualize a consciousness dance, a swirling vortex of energy inviting this other person to join me by exercising their free will, and then cocreate a shared energy connection for the purpose of communication. As we allow our consciousnesses into this vortex, we are drawn together, intermingled, and combined.

In this combined energetic form, I am suggesting two consciousnesses can communicate and exist together for the purposes of sharing anything from a spiritual to a physical experience. Eventually this temporary energetic form and shared consciousness dissolves and each consciousness returns to individual existence.

This sort of shared consciousness experience is just an example. I believe each one of us can visualize and manifest so much more with as much complexity as desired for the purposes of our soul growth, enlightenment, and communication.

Can this shared experience occur without my permission?

I tend to believe the answer is no, as long as I am aware of my ability to assert my free will to prevent a particular scenario. If I literally assert my free will to imagine an energy barrier to block out all nefarious attempts to manipulate my energy, I believe I can shut out such attempts such as remote influence and the like.

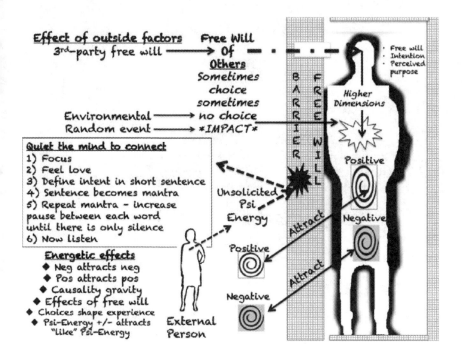

While remote influencers or others may attempt to direct energy with negative intent, each of us has the power to transmute ill will into loving energy that will not harm us.

All we must do is visualize and shape an energy shield with loving energy by tapping into the unlimited love energy of the universe to counter negative intended attacks. We can visualize energetic creations, shaped by our focused energy with intention to manifest, such as visualizing a shield.

Manifestation

Being an inventor all my life, I have used techniques to bring thought form into existence by way of my inventions. Does the inventing process of visualization first bring such thought into existence in an energetic form within the *space between the space*? Could this be why there are many stories of inventors inventing the same invention at the same moment in time?

Intention Creations

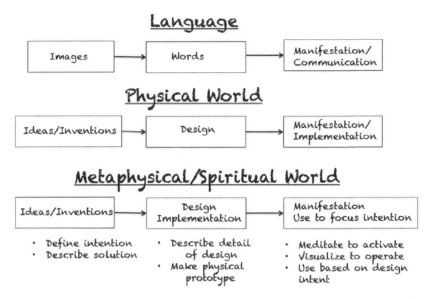

Examples of the intention of one or more souls to create include language, things in the physical world, and access to the spiritual world manifest from visualization and thought into the life experience of one or more incarnated souls within the physical world.

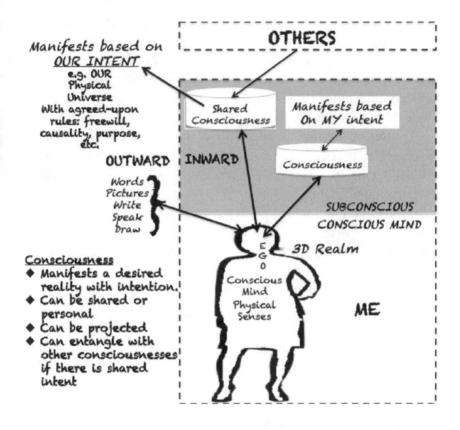

It is important to note that at times it is difficult to discern fact from fantasy and some may choose to believe such abilities are not possible. Regardless, only the individual incarnated soul who is experiencing the life moment can speak to the experience.

I trust my experiences by staying open and not allowing my conscious mind to interject or taint those experiences. I spend a great deal of time asking questions and working through experiences to determine what rings of truth and what does not. I stay open to the possibility that fantasy or other factors may taint my results, and I do my best to experiment and experience before reporting my perceptions on the metaphorical elephant's underbelly.

I also believe free will is a fundamental principle while incarnated in this present moment. However, when I apply my assumption of a free will universal principle to reports from experiencers regarding ETs, abduction, and the ETs manipulation of abductees, my theory breaks down.

Some experts in the field suggest that a soul agreement may have been made to allow such abductions. In numerous cases, subjects under deep hypnosis have confirmed such an agreement made during the prelife planning.

Before assuming a prelife planning agreement was put in place in all cases, there may be a combination of scenarios involved. One scenario may occur with ETs who use a combination of techniques including some form of physical trance-inducing technology coupled with a consciousness connection via the *space between the space*. They may even be able to insert screen memories and other such things using their technology. If that is the case, we should be able to reverse engineer how that technology works.

The ET abduction free will question requires further study and investigation. Here's an example ET question: if ETs on Earth are in fact using mind control or other physical manipulation to keep their presence secret, why can't we expand our consciousness to circumvent such manipulation by asserting our individual free will to thwart external influence and mind control? I realize questions such as this one may seem unknowable. But I say, ask big questions—the bigger, the better. One never knows what answers will come.

Cocreators

When I think of the *space between the space* as an energetic reflection of our 3D universe, I start to understand how thought and intention transform energy that manifests in the 3D universe and affects my life experience. I am not suggesting that we are superheroes ready to fly faster than a speeding train. Rather, I am suggesting we have much more influence over our life experience in this present moment than we realize.

I am suggesting that we have the power within us to visualize and apply this visualization in ways that can enhance our lives. For some, sitting down to meditate may be all that is needed. For most of us, we need more guidance to remove the limitations we have come to believe.

I think you already know how this works. Take, for example,

the use of prayer and meditation. Millions of people practice this approach every day.

Prayer and meditation are beautiful ways to focus one's intention to a particular challenge or situation. We ask for assistance with as much specificity as possible and envision an optimal outcome. Those approaches have provided many of us with tools to ask a higher power for guidance, wisdom, and solutions.

What else might we try? As an inventor, my inventions serve to solve problems. Such problems might relate to an industry need, a consumer desire, or even a better way to do something.

The process I use involves defining the problem I wish to solve in as much detail as possible, brainstorming ideas for how I might solve it, crafting a solution that solves the problem of interest, and then describing the invention in writing using the format required by patent offices around the world.

What if I used the same approach to solve problems applying the lessons I have learned about spirituality? How would I go about it?

Energetic Inventions

I would start by defining my intent with as much detail as possible. For example, this could be a statement such as I will not allow the negative energy of others to affect my life.

Sure, you could simply state this intention and meditate on it or pray about it. But what if you visualized a virtual device that redirects negative energy aimed at you to a virtual invention you define.

For example, you might visualize a single piece of pyrite crystal wrapped with silver wire and connected to three crystals where one crystal takes in the negative energy, uses the wound silver wire to transform the energy into positive energy, and outputs it using a second crystal to send positive energy back to the negative person. The third crystal may simply be used to provide you with connection to unlimited energy.

You might even create a physical prototype to help you visualize your invention. This is not to say such a prototype holds any power on its own; it is simply a representation of the invention you are visualizing within your mind to assist you in focusing your intention. You are shaping energy to function as you intend.

You don't have to make the process complex. You might simply wind a single crystal with silver wire and visualize it as a negative-to-positive energy converter. Sketch out your intention on paper or you may merely visualize it and activate it within your mind.

The process is only used to focus your intention in a meaningful way using imagery. The process is much like the use of language as described earlier. With language we have created words to represent physical and abstract things in our world as a means of communicating. We visualized a means of transportation with four wheels, an engine, and a covered place to operate it—we called this a car. Our visualizations manifest into the world around us and represent how we feel, think, and live. But words limit us too.

We can all be inventors who shape our life experience by simply identifying what we need in our life. We do this by focusing our intention and visualizing a virtual tool that will help us achieve our desired solution.

In some ways, this idea for focusing intention should give us confidence that we do have the ability to shape our lives as we wish them to be by asserting our free will and not infringing upon the free will of others.

The following process represents a summary of the steps for creating energetic inventions using a process of visualization and manifestation. I define this as the Intention Manifestation Protocol (IMP).

Intention Manifestation Protocol

- Define intention as specific as possible
- Visualize a virtual solution to facilitate intention
- Describe solution in detail using diagrams, language, pictures, sketches, photos, senses, etc.
- Build prototype if possible to assist in the visualization; it is only an aid (prop/symbolic/Icon) to use during meditation

- Meditate on specific intention while applying solution, e.g., energy transmutation, telepathic communication, remote viewing aid, etc.

- Solution acts as an amplifier of intention

In the next chapter, I will introduce a specific example to aid in the process of building and visualizing energetic creations.

Chapter 18
Energy Manifestation Invention

A single vibration emerged when the weight of nothing became something.
—R. E. Rowe

Given that each one of us exists in all dimensions simultaneously, it makes sense that intention is the backbone of awareness within a given dimension. As such, the idea of life in our present 3D universe translates into a shared consciousness experience with focused intention to experience physical existence.

Simply put, my intention in this moment is to experience this 3D realm with other incarnated souls who wish to share the experience. While the system framework for this particular Earth soul school has apparently been established for all incarnated souls, the workings of this Earth school, such as societies, cultures, economies, etc., evolve as a result of incarnated soul experiences and the real-time assertion of free will.

It is also reasonable to assume that scores of multidimensional entities work within the 3D realm to assist in its physical evolution. I experienced this during one of my regressions where I lived in another galaxy and was responsible for igniting new stars. I marveled as I used energetic tools to initiate the chain reaction resulting in one heck of a fireworks show!

Other entities assigned or drawn to a particular soul school may be responsible for assisting evolution within the 3D realm by way of tweaks needed to provide adequate physical bodies for future soul incarnations.

Reports by NDErs and from subjects in hypnotherapy

sessions indicate many of them experience a space between the 3D and 4D realms where experiencers often see their body from above during an NDE and hear conversations of people around their physical body.

This transitory realm, or buffer realm, is what I have termed the "*space between the space.*" It is where I believe our consciousness accesses information, connects with other consciousnesses to communicate, and travels in energetic form (such as astral travel).

It is further reasonable to assume this to be the realm where our consciousness can gather, shape, and work with energy to interact with the physical world. Additionally, I have come to believe it is the same realm where energy organizes itself by way of our intention. In other words, the very existence of this in-between realm enables incarnated souls to manifest an intention by shaping energy to assist our life experience within the 3D world. This feels like the same process I have used all of my life as an inventor.

From an inventor's mindset, I see a problem and intend to solve it. I imagine possible solutions then sketch and describe possible solutions in my notebook using language and diagrams. As solutions to my well-defined problem emerge, I break down the embodiment of my solution into individual components to enable someone skilled in the art to build it. It is the process required to obtain a US patent. Most of these ideas may come from the workings of my physical brain and my present life experience, but other aspects of the ideas and inspirations may come to me from the Divine Library and the *space between the space*.

After documenting a typical invention, I reduce it to practice by using a combination of software (computer code) and hardware to shape my invention into a physical thing able to function as I intend in the 3D world to solve the identified problem.

I wondered if I could use a similar process to design energetic inventions to solve particular life experience problems? How could I manifest such inventions using energy? How could I convert what I perceive as negative energy impacting my life into loving energy?

I decided to start by identifying a governing principle— applying my free will. I must also assume this means there are personal consequences if I violate the free will of someone else without their permission. Similarly, to protect myself from any kind of harmful or negative energy all I need to do is proclaim my intention that any negative external energy with nefarious intent will not be allowed to affect me or anyone around me. Asserting my intention to protect myself is like putting up an instantaneous force field to shut out negative energy—shields up! It is much like a firewall used to protect a computer, shutting out hackers.

Building on this idea of imagining a force field or firewall, the act of imagining such a thing invokes my intention and shapes the energy around my energetic body (I think of my energy body as an energetic reflection of my 3D body, existing in the *space between the space*).

My intention shapes energy into the creation I imagine that will assist me during my life experience. Shaping energy does not mean I can make money appear out of nothing, but it just might explain why some people can bend spoons, receive remote viewing information, dowse, and so on.

Building upon these ideas, it then becomes reasonable to assume there is no physical energy in geometric shapes, crystals, letters, or writing without my intention for it to exist. Energy associated with such things originates from my intention or interpretation of intention related to such geometric shapes, crystals, letters, or writing.

As suggested, it is important to note that attempting to use intention to affect another soul negatively affects the one trying such things. Each one of us should recognize we have the power of our free will to turn away apparent attempts to manipulate us with negative energy in any form. All I need to do is to make my intention clear by saying something like *I will block out negative energy trying to affect me.*

To build on this idea that I can shape energy by way of my thought, I can either use this thought process to attract those things to me that I believe I need in my life or I can use something physical to represent or symbolize my intention.

For example, I may wish to (1) visualize a vibration of love, (2) write the word love to convey such an intention, resulting in the energetic formation of love, or (3) create a symbol such as a heart icon to express a loving intention. A love vibration is formed by way of my intention as I use any one of these three approaches within the *space between the space.*

The next step in this example is to direct that love vibration or energy. This can be accomplished by my implied intention (1) wanting to feel the love energy, (2) wanting to share the love energy, or (3) spontaneously feeling the love energy as the result of a random thought, physical experience, a moment of empathy, or a distant memory.

As I think deeper about these ideas, it is reasonable to assume that early human symbolic languages memorialized in pictograms and glyphs may have been created to shape intention.

Additionally, if the incarnated soul sets their intention to share their energetic creation as depicted in a pictogram or glyph with other incarnated souls, these other incarnated souls can assert their free will to share the experience of the energy represented in the pictogram or glyph. Continuing with the love energy example, I can say, *when I look at a picture of a heart, I experience feelings of love.*

This same approach applies to physical things. For example, I can choose to share the belief of others that crystals have power or I can choose to believe that my intention to represent a specific kind of energy or vibration, such as healing, is represented by a particular type of crystal that embodies my intentions. Thus the natural crystal becomes a physical symbol of my intention.

It is easy for most of us to look at a physical thing and associate it with some presumed functionality. But the real truth is that physical things only *represent* the energy we give them. A reflection of this physical symbol then exists as energy in the *space between the space* where it can interact with other energy reflections.

Now I understand how I am able to manifest my reality by way of energy formations within this in-between realm. The process is not good or bad. It is merely how the universe works based on the nature of shared consciousness, intention, and free will. Additionally, I can say I am a cocreator in this 3D realm.

How can I test these ideas? How can I use these insights to improve my life experience?

I can use the age-old tradition of prayer to clarify my intention. I can meditate while focusing on my intention. I can even use a customized approach to focus my intention. This customized approach might be through the use of a meaningful sound, mantra, word, sentence, image, picture, or series of pictures that represents my intention.

What if I use language to focus my intention? I could write down my intention utilizing written words or I could create a symbolic language by creating glyphs or pictograms that represent my intention.

Again, it is important to note I am using this process only as a tool to focus my intention. The power is not in my creation. The power comes from my intention, which focuses energy and enables it to take shape for use in my life.

How would a symbolic language tool to shape energy work? Refer to the glyphs I created in Appendix D.

The following describes my energetic invention:

- I defined each glyph as having a specific energetic functionality.

- I assembled these glyphs one symbol at a time to represent my intention.

- Once assembled, I am able to look upon the series of glyphs and focus my intention to shape the energy represented by the glyphs to function as intended.

I have created a personal energy-shaping invention aimed at assisting me in my life. Now someone might say I have an excellent imagination, or someone may tell me I have just described my intention to explain what I need to help me with my life in this moment.

The series of glyphs below form a pictograph, which is a description of the energetic invention I have created by way of my focused intention. In this example, I imagine I wish to heal myself in some way by collecting violet (healing) energy, amplify that energy, shower myself in it, and then feel waves of love. Finally, I output those feelings of love back to spiritual realms.

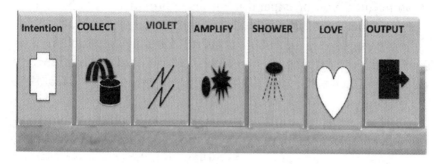

As shown above, I move through the pictogram one glyph at a time or I can draw each glyph into a pictogram as illustrated below. By visualizing and setting my intention, I can enable my energetic invention to provide the desired functionality. Remember all these symbols do is represent my intention. It is like writing out my intention in a condensed way.

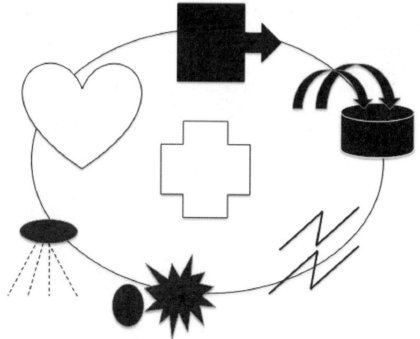

Now try creating your own glyphs using shapes that are meaningful to you or expand upon those provided in Appendix D. Combine the glyphs into something important and personalized. Next, use your imagination to visualize a problem then configure your glyphs to visualize each part of a solution. By visualizing each part of the solution, focus your intention to manifest the illustrated solution.

You have the spiritual power to manifest whatever you feel you need in this moment to make life more joyful by way of shaping the energy reflections of the 3D world within the *space between the space.*

I think of this approach as a way to shape my prayers and focus the intent of my meditation. While I often pray using words like I have done since I was a child, there are times I want to enhance my prayers with images and emotion such as the examples in this chapter.

This process of creating glyphs and pictographs gives me a tool to enhance language by combining words, emotion, context, and meaning in order to convey very specific intent. The process becomes very personal and helps me to visualize and focus on a particular challenge or issue. It can sometimes pull me out of a funk and helps me remember I am a cocreator of my lifetime experience.

By no means does the process replace prayer for me. Rather, I feel as if my prayers have more meaning and clarity. Most of all have fun with this approach or use another approach that works for you.

Chapter 19
Affirmations

Affirmations are an easy way to remind us that we can shape our perspective of the world, connect to spiritual realms, and enhance our life experience.

This does not mean the physical me is creating a parallel universe or standing alone from other incarnated souls. I believe we are using a personal approach to our spiritual connection using descriptive sentences that have meaning.

This approach enables me to apply my connection with higher dimensions and brighten my life experience in this dimension.

Some may believe this idea is the same as creating a personal version of reality. There is some truth in that perspective. However, I think of it as more of a personal approach to spirituality, empowering me to apply personal insights to daily life.

Rather than latching onto something I do not fully comprehend, I expand my beliefs to include unlimited possibilities, miracles, and a personal responsibility to shape my life experience by asserting free will.

How do you feel about what I wrote above? Do you agree? Do you disagree? What are your thoughts? Write out how you feel in your notebook. Describe your spiritual beliefs.

There are no right or wrong ways to describe your beliefs. It is personal and your perspective. Realize each of us has a place on the metaphoric elephant and a unique perspective regarding connection to spiritual realms.

It is remarkable when doubt fades, and understanding deepens, knowing we are connected with an unlimited source of love. However, awareness of connectedness does not mean that life will be easy or without challenge.

Knowing there is more beyond our self provides confidence and reassurance. It can motivate us to put one foot in front of the other when our life journey takes a turn through a field of mud. We keep moving. We do our best, set boundaries, lovingly assert free will, and visualize our hope for the future.

Pray, meditate, or focus your intention in whatever way feels right to you. Personally connect to spiritual realms and feel the love that comes with the connection.

Trust the field of mud will transform into a lovely meadow. It takes effort, but you will find joy. Believe it.

Here are some affirmations I use when life becomes difficult. Use these affirmations or create a list of your own. Pray, meditate, and focus your intention.

▶ I will stay open, trust my gut, and believe I am connected to love.

▶ I give myself permission to experience the life I want.

▶ I empower myself to believe that which I cannot see, hear, or touch.

▶ I will work hard during my life experience to love, learn, and trust in spiritual realms while asserting my free will with love.

▶ I have free will. All other incarnated souls around me have free will too.

▶ I must remember when events out of my control occur that my wants and desires may not be aligned with the wants and desires of other incarnated souls around me.

▶ Timing is just as important as intention. Both must be aligned.

▶ Loss hurts, but it is momentary. Love is forever.

▶ I will learn from my experiences and keep love in my heart throughout the process.

▶ I can forgive without being passive to another person's free will that might be in conflict with my own free will.

▶ I will continue to be in difficult situations until I learn the intended lessons.

▶ There is an infinite amount of information accessible by focusing my intent and desire to receive specific information from spiritual realms.

▶ Loving spiritual entities are available to assist me when I need help.

▶ The miracle of physical existence and the opportunity to experience is what brings me to this Earth school.

▶ I am unique and alive at this moment for an important reason.

▶ I have heavenly support. I am not alone.

▶ I will ask for spiritual assistance when I need help and keep love at the center of my requests.

▶ I will keep moving forward with love and search for my personal perspective of truth.

▶ I will listen to the silence and fill comforted.

▶ I will put one foot in front of the other. I will breathe in and out until I feel doubt pass.

▶ I CAN do this life thing!

▶ Love and intuition will guide me.

▶ I will embrace every moment.

▶ I do not need to travel anywhere. I exist within higher dimensions. Higher dimensions are all around me.

▶ I am blessed. I will do my best.

▶ I will think big and work hard.

Chapter 20
Lessons Learned

The writing of this second book has been an incredible learning experience. I had always felt connected to spiritual realms, but I had no idea there was an information source available to answer my questions.

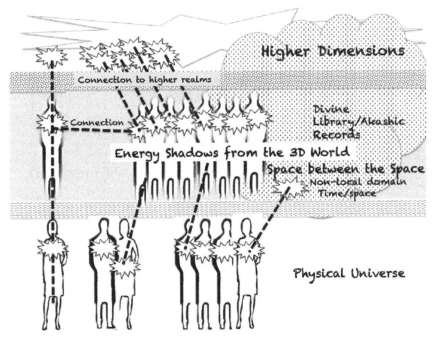

I now have a better understanding of how NDErs can experience a life playback and where subjects under deep hypnosis go when they refer to a spiritual library. I learned about spiritual teachers and channels who work with their clients to address life challenges by accessing soul-specific information in the Divine Library, sometimes referred to as the Akashic Records.

I found an infinite amount of information accessible by focusing my intent and desire to receive specific information by sending out requests while meditating, praying, under hypnosis, or with focused intention as I sketched in my notebook.

I became aware of loving spiritual entities available to assist me with the information I request and help me as I continue on this spiritual journey. I discovered how to visualize and project my consciousness while opening up to receive information, interpret responses, and assert my free will to embrace my life experience.

I had not considered the idea that language shaped my perception of reality and shaped the physical world around me. It was a real eye-opener. I confirmed that while each of us has one or more purpose(s), there are also shared, group-oriented lessons to be learned.

It became clear to me that group participation is a wonderful way to shape our physical world into the world we collectively want it to be. We can transform our world into a soul school for learning with minimal suffering and enhanced joy by asserting our free will with support from spiritual realms to accomplish whatever we collectively desire.

I learned about the field of parapsychology and discovered the protocols of remote viewing and dowsing with rods and pendulums, both of which I am eager to learn more from experts as I continue on my journey.

I experimented with telepathy and found I have much more to learn, experience, and explore. I created energetic inventions as a way to manifest what I feel I need in my lifetime. I even developed an example using customized wood pieces and pictograms. I learned how to shape energy by visualizing the *space between the space* and creating energetic inventions to help me with my life. I learned there were many ways to focus my intention for different objectives.

FOCUS	INTENTION
OBE	Higher Dimension Discovery/Observation spiritual growth and understanding, explore
Past-Life Regression/ NDE	Review/Study of past lives for personal soul growth, understanding, and learning
Between-life hypnotherapy Spontaneous OBE	Study of Earth school/healing/life planning for spiritual growth and understanding
Meditation, Prayer	Connection to higher dimensions for healing, energy, balancing, etc.
Divine Library Access (Akashic Records)	Learning with higher dimensional spiritual support
Dowsing/Remote Viewing	Answering questions/collecting information
Channeling	Connection to external consciousness

I hope this book inspires you to dig deeper and find personal meaning in spiritual topics that interest you. Perhaps my process and the ideas presented will motivate and excite you about the spiritual wonders available to everyone. I am hopeful that my books will help readers on their spiritual journey realize we all have the ability to deepen our spiritual connection by merely visualizing and feeling the love that comes with it.

No matter what challenges one has in their life, the miracle of physical existence and the opportunity to learn is what keeps bringing us back to this Earth school by way of reincarnation. Additionally, I hope after reading this book I have helped you embrace the fact that you are unique and alive at this moment for an important reason.

Believe this to be true.

Trust you will find your purpose if you are seeking answers. No matter how difficult life has become, trust that you have heavenly support.

You are not alone.

Format your questions for the Divine Library in your personal notebook. Ask for spiritual assistance. Be specific. Keep love at the center of your requests with any actions you decide to take. Believe you will receive answers and insights you need to succeed.

Be prepared to receive responses when you least expect them and remember timing plays a critical role in the overall experience of incarnated souls. Just keep moving forward and searching for your truth.

You may not feel the incredible love around you, but believe me when I say it is always present. Every now and then, open up and listen to the silence. Breathe in and imagine warm spiritual vibrations filling you with the strength you need to keeping moving forward.

Get back to learning lessons with a positive attitude by moving one foot in front of the other. Breathe in again and again until your doubts fade.

I can do this. Say it out loud, if you feel unsure. I can do this. Say it again, but louder: I can do this!

Put your Ego in a time-out.

Become inspired to learn. Let love and intuition guide you and embrace your life experience. Higher dimensions may feel impossible to grasp, so keep your connection and dialog to spiritual realms pure and simple.

Try to remember that you do not need to go anywhere. You exist within all dimensions simultaneously. Spiritual realms are all around you.

If you are still on the fence about going on your own spiritual journey, just take a chance. Start small.

As you gain more confidence, you will discover you are on the most exciting adventure of your life!

Get motivated to move beyond the comfort of your personal fish bowl and explore an infinite ocean of possibility.

No one is ever too old to learn, dream big, or discover. Stay tuned as this never-ending spiritual journey continues. I wish you many amazing spiritual adventures.

Richard Rowe

Appendix A

Regression Experiences with the Library
Interview with Scott Fitzgerald De Tamble

Scott Fitzgerald De Tamble, CHt, is a clinical hypnotherapist in Southern California specializing in past-life regression and Life Between Lives® spiritual regression. Trained in 2004 by Dr. Michael Newton in Newton's Life Between Lives® hypnotic method, Scott has since guided over a thousand *Life Between Lives®* sessions.

Life Between Lives® is a profound hypnotherapy technique in which clients connect with their own soul awareness. Guided into the spiritual state between physical lifetimes, clients can meet and communicate with their own Spirit Guides, greet their beloved soul mates and soul groups, and consult advanced spiritual masters known as Elders. They may also have various experiences such as communicating with crossed-over loved ones, visiting places of healing, and doing research in the Divine Library, an area of information where what is sometimes referred to as the Akashic Records may be consulted and studied.

Richard Rowe (RR): *How common is it for your subjects to discuss a Divine Library or bring it up?*

Scott: Perhaps one out of twelve or so of my clients may spontaneously visit the library in their Life Between Lives® (LBL) sessions. Others may be led or directed there by their Spirit Guides, teachers, or other spiritual beings that we may encounter. Some clients express a specific desire to visit the library before their session begins, and we are usually able to fulfill their request to enjoy that experience.

RR: *What sort of information do your subjects indicate is in the library?*

S: The vast majority of clients in my sessions visit the library in order to study their own soul history, focusing for the most part on their past lives, their previous physical incarnations. This study will often include looking at the past lifetime that we may have just visited some time earlier during their LBL session. We may view key points in the current lifetime as well, usually moments leading up to where they now stand.

Soul histories may include their creation as individual beings, their activities as "baby souls" before beginning their incarnations, their lives on Earth and possibly on other physical and nonphysical worlds, and all spirit time in between lifetimes.

RR: *What other key elements of the library have you learned from your subjects?*

S: LBL sessions are rather lengthy, often running three to four hours or more. As mentioned, clients may have many and diverse experiences within a session, but a visit to the library can often bring that special insight that opens new avenues and opportunities.

Because of the existence and accessibility of their own soul histories, people are able to gain a higher perspective of the goals, purposes, activities, relationships, and challenges in the current lifetime. With this longer view, we can often spot recurring themes and patterns throughout their lifetimes, and thus more clearly understand the portent of whatever dramas may be transpiring in the here and now.

In reading about, viewing, or immersing into a previous lifetime's records, clients are able not only to review their own experiences, but are also able to understand the impact they may have had on other people, and on subsequent events. Knowledge acquired in our visits to the library often inspires a person to make more beneficial choices and actions in their current life.

There is much more to the library, but this is how we tend to utilize it in our LBL sessions.

RR: *Have you come across any discussion of information in the library that is not soul-specific? That is, of a more general nature?*

S: Yes. Some clients have indicated that the library contains information on the general history of Earth, other planets, star systems, and galaxies that souls may have incarnated within and cosmological information about the creation and history of the entire universe.

I've had a few clients access technical knowledge in their chosen fields of science, engineering, physics, medicine, and other areas of study.

There is also information on ethics, philosophy, systems of thought, emotion, behavior, and so many things. As far as I can tell, the library is pretty much a cornucopia of knowledge and records, a sort of super-Wikipedia of Everything.

The library seems to hold information on everything that has ever existed or occurred on every dimension, including thoughts, feelings, dreams, animal, vegetable, mineral, Devic kingdoms, spiritual, angelic, perhaps even motions of atoms . . . it's all recorded. You might say the library is "God's Memory."

RR: *Do there appear to be spiritual entities who are dedicated to managing all aspects of the library?*

S: Yes, there are various managers, teachers, and support workers in the library. There is often a "greeter" or librarian who meets us when we approach, welcoming and directing us to what we may want to explore (although sometimes we may just wander in on our own). There are counselors, who will sit down with souls and help them to study and understand their lives and records. There are archivists, who bustle about and seem to focus on sorting or managing the Records. I imagine there are also very advanced souls behind the scenes who plan, direct, and manage what must be an infinitely complex system.

An intriguing aspect is that, in our sessions, and perhaps also in other methods of accessing the records, these librarians or record keepers always seem to know that we're coming! We are welcomed and directed to certain areas where we are presented with the very materials we are looking for, or just what we "need" to find in that moment.

RR: *For those subjects who have experienced the library, did they have a role or duty associated with the library? If so, what was it?*

S: I do recall a specific LBL session some years ago in which my client played a role. As soon as we entered the "between lives" or spirit world portion of the session, she, as a soul, made a beeline to return to the library, to continue work on some project there. She was quite eager to get back to it. Apparently, she was/is a library worker of a certain type, a sort of archivist who organized and prepared information, and there seemed to be a group enterprise she was involved in, together with some associates. She was very knowledgeable about the inner workings of the library, and felt very much at home there. We explored her project a bit, and then moved on to focus on other spiritual activities. Not surprisingly, in her current lifetime she is rather comfortable around books and information.

RR: *Does the library always look the same as in distinct characteristics or does it vary from subject to subject?*

S: A majority of my clients have perceived the library as a monumental building with Classical architecture, similar to what we might find in ancient Greece or Rome. Columns, wide marble- like stairways leading up, huge doors, vast and seemingly endless halls and rooms, with tiers and tiers, rows upon rows of books and other media organized and ensconced.

There are usually many, many tables or desks occupied by countless other souls engaged in doing research of their own. They seldom if ever interact with my clients, other than perhaps a passing nod of acquaintance or acknowledgment here or there. They are intensely immersed in their own studies. Various library workers may be seen here and there, supporting other souls in their quests for information. And so most of my clients perceive this spiritual storehouse of information as simply "a library," in human terms, if a rather grand one.

There are those clients who perceive things a bit differently. It's important to remember that, in our sessions, my clients are perceiving what is essentially energy or light, through the lens of a human brain or mind. To make sense of it all, and to be able to communicate about it, we tend to clothe the energy in earthly terms or forms that we can understand. Or, perhaps, our Spirit Guides or those library personnel may create and project these forms into our human minds and awareness. But a few clients have seen the library in what I think may be its true form, which again is light and energy. They see themselves, for that matter, not in human body or appearance, but as pulsating or vibrating light forms that may be vaguely human shaped; or often, as colorful orb-like spheres of light/energy.

We do sometimes perceive or imagine the library almost as a physical building or space/location to which we must travel, gain entrance, and arrive. But, much as our present-day cellphones are in constant contact with a network through which we can access the Internet at any time, I believe we can communicate with and even download the library's information from any location—if our consciousness is tuned to the right frequency.

RR: *Is the subject matter always present in book form? Or are there rooms where souls go to view too? Any other playback features that are interesting?*

S: As mentioned, sometimes clients are met and counseled and taught by library counselors, who communicate with the client, showing them and teaching them, helping them to understand particular information. Also, a person's own Spirit Guide(s) may lead them and show what is meant to be shown, discussing this with the person (and myself as bystander and questioner).

Other times, clients are given free rein to explore a body of information all on their own.

It is very common for my clients to be led to a space where there is a table featuring a large "Book of Life"—the client's past life, current life, or Book of All Lives. It is often presented as a beautiful leather-bound tome, perhaps eighteen to twenty inches tall, several inches thick, with gilded cover, etc. A book may be graced with the person's name in fancy glowing lettering as the title. A person can open and read the book as words, or sometimes there are living and moving images in the pages, akin to movies being played. Sometimes it feels as if these Books of Life are alive themselves, as they may open or jump to certain pages or information. There have been times when the books go only so far, so many chapters, and then there are blank pages—pages that are to remain unknown at the time of our visit. Or, perhaps they are blank in order to leave space for the person to "write" the rest of their current life.

Oftentimes, rather than books, information is simply viewed on video screens, one or many; or sometimes the life movies are projected into the middle of the room as clear and defined holographic images that may be viewed from different angles.

I recall a session in which my client perceived a column about four feet tall in the center of a room, and atop the column hovered a large crystal ball. In the crystal was glimpsed moving images of lifetime activities, past and present.

In most of these forms, the information is not only visual, but also a fully immersive experience in which all other senses come into play, including thought and emotion. That is, people can see, hear, feel, smell, taste, and just know and understand all of what is occurring. They can also read between the lines to understand the connections between the actions shown, their soul's greater path, and their current human existence.

Some people may touch a mist hanging in the air, or a light, or just walk into a room, and experience direct torrential downloads or dumps of information, all at once. They may be conscious of the information and able to describe and share it with me; or sometimes they are not consciously aware of the information that has been given to them, as it has been packed away inside of them for future use at some strategic time.

My impression is that the form a library experience takes has a direct connection with the consciousness and needs of the client at that moment.

RR: *What other insights have you gained from your subjects with respect to the library?*

S: I believe that we have each been gifted with a "library card," and are welcome to access the records. That range of access, however, is keyed to our level of development, awareness, intent, and needs of the moment. The librarians, and the library itself, seem, if not omniscient, very aware of who we are, what we're looking for, and the appropriateness of our request for information.

There seem to be built-in safeguards regarding what types of information we may access at certain points in our journey. The library will not allow itself to be used to preempt or interfere with one's desired self-learning through life experiences-to-come. It will not reveal sensitive information to someone with negative or self-aggrandizing motives.

I have seen it show various possibilities, and track possible outcomes of actions or decisions, and in that way, it can be used as a tool for thought and study. I do not believe it will, or even can, show the absolute future per se, as that is for us to create. In fact, we are ourselves adding to the library in every moment, with our thoughts, feelings, and actions. And so in that sense, it is indeed a living resource, constantly growing and evolving.

RR: *Would you say the library is of key importance to soul study and between-life training?*

S: Absolutely. It seems absolutely essential. Time and time again in LBL sessions, we experience moments when my client is involved in some study of the records, whether alone or with their soul group, teachers/guides, council, or some other wise being. As a lifetime is lived, it is recorded, and then later studied very intensely in spirit, especially by the soul who lived it.

They comb through these precious lifetimes for moments of decision, analyzing the thoughts, feelings, and motives that led to that decision. They look at the activities and outcomes, experiencing this from many different perspectives, including those of the people, far and near, who may have been affected. They explore possible alternate decisions or events, and discuss these with their teachers and friends.

Several of one's lifetimes may be studied in sequence to discern patterns and themes, with an eye at looking toward the overall development of the soul. Is it learning? Is it growing and expanding? What are its long-term goals for self-development, and for contributing to the All?

So, yes, the library does indeed provide an excellent resource for the continuing evolution of souls. It is a universal treasury that we all create and that we all share.

Scott Fitzgerald De Tamble, C. Ht., LBL website: lightbetweenlives. com

NOTE: LIFE BETWEEN LIVES is a registered trademark by The Michael Newton Institute for Life Between Lives Hypnotherapy, Inc. in Wilmington, NC, 28404.

Appendix B

Interfacing with the Divine Library
Quick Reference Guide

The process for interfacing with the Divine Library is a very personal experience. As such, you must discover what works for you. To start the process off, you can meditate, pray, or simply focus and quiet your mind.

My approach is to have a conversation inside my head with spiritual realms without speaking. Start by being thankful for blessings in your life. Next, explain the situation and why you need assistance.

Follow or modify the steps below to suit your personal needs:

1. Trust the information you are seeking exists; be open-minded to the notion that the inquiry will be heard and the desired information is available.

2. Visualize the category of information where answers will be located. To receive information related to your inquiry, visualize the data is stored in the Divine Library and is available to you.

3. Quiet your mind. Use the same techniques utilized by self-hypnosis, prayer, and meditation. Send out a loving prayer for, or meditate on, receiving guidance from spiritual realms.

4. Define exactly what knowledge or insights are desired; focus intently on receiving a response to your inquiry.

5. Take notes in a notebook of what impressions come to you. As thoughts, feelings, and ideas arrive related to your inquiry, document what comes to you using words and sketches. Write it all down without editing or judgment.

6. After a time, review your notes and interpret them. Review

the information you have written down and attempt to understand the information. Determine how it relates to your inquiry. How can the received information make your life better?

7. Sketching example:

✓ Use a notepad or a word processor on a computer.
✓ Write down questions.

✓ Clear your mind and fill it with love and compassion.

✓ Let ideas flow into your mind.
✓ Sketch out or write notes about the things that come to you.

✓ Pay particular attention to how the incoming thoughts make you feel.

✓ How do the ideas make you feel?

Appendix C

Brainstorming Purpose
Quick Reference Guide

Write three things for each list as quickly as you can. Do not over think or edit.

List 1. Things I like to do.
List 2. If I could have any job in the world what would it be?
List 3. What are my current hobbies?
List 4. What gets me upset?
List 5. What makes me laugh?
List 6. The last time I was late for something, I was doing this.

Now take your lists and put an asterisk next to the top item in each list. For example, in list one, which one of the three things you wrote down do you like to do best? That is the one you circle. Use the asterisked or circled item from each list to fill in this sentence:

I would like to do [List1] while working as a [List2] and doing [List3] during my free time, but I want to avoid [List4] and laugh while [List5] as long as I am not [List6] because I will be late.

Here is an example of how your brainstorming of purpose might look:

Brainstorming Purpose

List 1
write
Research
Play guitar

List 2
hypnotherapist
writer
photographer

List 3
hiking
Taking pictures
traveling

List 4
bad customer service
Red Tape
Wasting time

List 5
Playing with the grandkids
Playing with golden retriever
Being a klutz

List 6
writing
self hypnosis
reading
watching a movie

Fill in the blanks

I would like to do [List1] while working as a [List2] and doing [List3] during my free time, but I want to avoid [List4] and laugh while [List5] as long as I am not [List6] because I will be late.

I would like to do **RESEARCH** while working as a **HYPNOTHERAPIST** and doing **HIKING** during my free time, but I want to avoid **Red Tape** and laugh while **PLAYING WITH THE GRANDKIDS** as long as I am not **WRITING** because I will be late.

Appendix D

Energetic Manifestation Invention Examples

Individual glyphs with specific meaning are listed within the following tables. To assemble the glyphs into an energetic system, start by defining your intention using one of the intention glyphs. Next, assemble your energetic system invention by imagining each glyph functioning as it connects the glyph next to it. A pictograph is formed from your series of glyphs to provide the intended functionality within the energy realm also known as the space between the space. To activate it, visualize each glyph functioning in the order intended.

Finally, draw a pictograph and imagine it as a fully functioning energy creation to aid you in your desired intention.

Glyphs – Pictograph Examples

 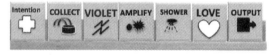

Intent to heal: collect violet energy, amply it, shower in it, feel the love, and output it back to the universe.

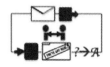 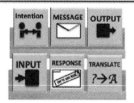

Intent to communicate with remote consciousness: form a message and send it out. Input a response and translate.

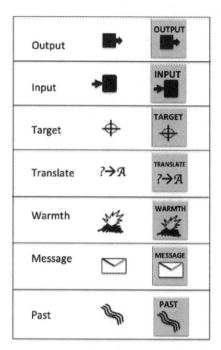

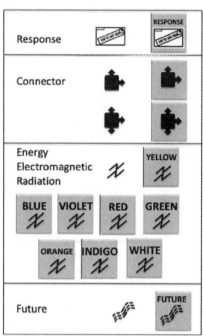

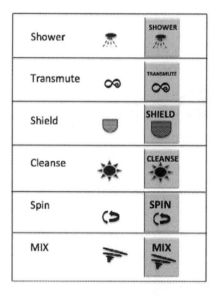

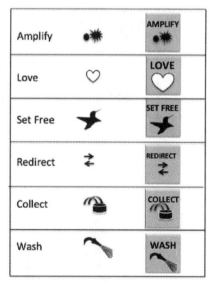

Intention

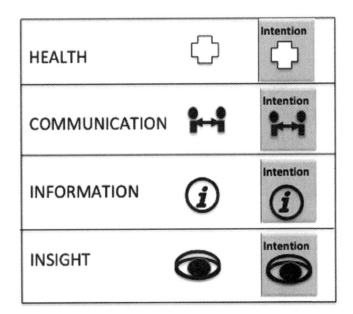

HEALTH	✛	Intention ✛
COMMUNICATION	🏋	Intention 🏋
INFORMATION	ⓘ	Intention ⓘ
INSIGHT	👁	Intention 👁

Intention Examples

HEALTH	I intend to heal myself or another using energy. Define the specific healing intention and intended outcome.
COMMUNICATION	I intend to communicate with another consciousness. Define the consciousness, visualize. Now visualize the message and intention to receive an answer.
INFORMATION	I intend to collect or gather information. Define the specific information of interest. Define why the information is needed.
INSIGHT	I intend to learn something specific. Define the specific lesson of interest. Define how receiving such an insight will assist your life experience.

Shower	Visualize energy raining on you as if taking a shower	Amplify	Amplify energy, allowing it to expand, grow and spread
Transmute	Change energy from one vibration to another	Love	Love vibration in its entirety physically and emotionally
Shield	Block external energy or external intention	Set Free	Send away something defined energetically or emotionally
Cleanse	Purify and remove unwanted energy, emotions, desires	Redirect	Reroute energy or intention from here to there
Spin	Spin energy to aid in combining or transmutation	Collect	Gather energy from the unlimited source
Mix	Mix a combination of energies to assist with a desired intention	Wash	Move out the undesired and cleanse the remaining

Output	Output energy as intended
Input	Input energy as intended
Target	Specify a specific location, object, place, consciousness, etc. in time and space
Translate	Convert information received into information understood
Warmth	Feel comforting warmth like being wrapped in a warm blanket
Message	Define a specific message with the intent to send it to a defined target

Response	Receive a specific message with the intent to translate and understand it
Connector	Route the flow of your energetic invention to add complexity and additional functionality
Past	Past time waves in the *space between the space*
Future	Future time waves in the *space between the space*

Energy
Electromagnetic Radiation Vibration

WHITE

Combination of all colors and energetic vibrations

 RED — This energy vibration is full of emotions from love to anger and can excite and energize. This vibration can intensify passion and feelings of safety.

 Orange — This energy vibration evokes warmth and represents abundance and harmony.

 Yellow — This energy vibration evokes feelings of happiness, joy, and hope. Use it to boost courage, optimism, and confidence.

 Green — This energy vibration evokes feelings of nature and the environment. It represents youth, renewal and fertility.

 Blue— This energy vibration evokes feelings of peace and tranquility, refreshing water. Use it to calm, refresh, and assist in communication.

 Indigo — This energy vibration evokes feelings of faith, existence within the vast cosmic consciousness, and the inner mind. Use it to increase depth of understanding and comprehension of thoughts and feelings.

 Violet — This energy vibration evokes healing of mind, body and spirit, awareness of being and spirituality. Use it to intensify connection with spirit.

Accessing
The Space Between the Space

- Shutting off the conscious mind/silence thought
  - Meditation, hypnosis, deep breathing. Focus away from the body, ritual, routine, distraction, avoid synthetic numbness (ie drugs, alcohol)
  - Love
- Visualize intention (mantra, chant, affirmations, solidified in someway)
- Focus deeper - Let feelings of love fill you
- Collect desired information
- Translating received information by way of our brain into words, images, and context
- Remembering the meaning behind information
- Releasing—Turn back on the conscious mind

Appendix F

Intention Manifestation Protocol ✦✦ (IMP) ✦✦

- Define intention as specific as possible
- Visualize a virtual solution to facilitate Intention
- Describe solution in detail using diagrams, language, pictures, sketches, photos, etc.
- Build prototype if possible to assist in the visualization - it is only an aid (prop/ symbolic/Icon) to use during meditation
- Meditate on specific intention while applying solution, e.g. energy transmutation, telepathic communication, remote viewing aid, etc.
- Solution acts as an amplifier of intention

IMP Protocol just an example of what each of us can do

References

Abbott, Edwin A. May 25, 2012. *Flatland [illustrated]*. Art & Poetry Publishing. Kindle Edition.

Abrams, Douglas, et al. 2016. *The Book of Joy*. New York: Avery. 145.

ADC Project. *After-Death Communications*. Retrieved on March 4, 2018, from http://www.after- death.com/.

Braden, Gregg. 2000. *The Isaiah Effect-Decoding the Lost Science of Prayer and Prophecy*. New York: Three Rivers Press. 146–47.

Cannon, Dolores. 1993. *Between Death and Life: Newly Updated and Revised Edition*, 13th printing. Huntsville, AR: Ozark Mountain Publishing. 90.

Cannon, Dolores. 2011. *The Three Waves of Volunteers and the New Earth*. Huntsville, AR: Ozark Mountain Publishing. 9–11.

Chyan, Jiyuh. 2017. *Your Key to the Akashic Records*. McLean, VA: Difference Press. 21.

De Tamble, Scott Fitzgerald. 2018. *Light Between Lives: The Loving Wisdom of Spirit*. Retrieved on March 1, 2018, from http://www.lightbetweenlives.com/about_lbl/spirit_guides.html.

De Tamble, Scott Fitzgerald. 2018. *Light Between Lives: Library and Life Selection*. Retrieved on March 25, 2018, from http://lightbetweenlives.com/about_lbl/library_life_selection.html.

Guggenheim, Bill, and Judy Guggenheim. 1995. *Hello from Heaven!*

A New Field of Research— After-Death-Communication—Confirms Life and Love Are Eternal. New York: Bantam Books.

Hein, Simeon. 2010. "Learn Remote Viewing Step 1: The Cool Down." Retrieved on March 17, 2018, from https://www.youtube.com/watch?v=mMws4s8PBXg.

Hein, Simeon. 2010. "Learn Remote Viewing Step 2: Connecting with the Signal Line." Retrieved on March 17, 2018, from https://www.youtube.com/watch?v=TSf0UzG-scg.

Hein, Simeon. 2010. "Learn Remote Viewing Step 3: Tuning into the Target's Resonance." Retrieved on March 17, 2018, from https://www.youtube.com/watch?v=GDDunSxIRpk.

Hein, Simeon. 2010. "Learn Remote Viewing Step 4: Opening the Aperture." Retrieved on March 17, 2018, from https://www.youtube.com/watch?v=zBFDxp0emV0.

Hein, Simeon. 2010. "Learn Remote Viewing Step 5: Closing the Session." Retrieved on March 17, 2018, from https://www.youtube.com/watch?v=OfAStNZqJQ0&t=367s.

Holden, J. M., B. Greyson, and D. James. 2009. *The Handbook of Near-Death Experiences: Thirty Years of Investigation.* Santa Barbara, CA: Praeger. 45–46, 229.

Howe, Linda. 2010. *How to Read the Akashic Records: Accessing the Archive of the Soul and Its Journey.* Boulder, CO: Sounds True. 11–12.

Hubbard, Scott G., and Gary O. Langford. 1986. *A Suggested Remote Viewing Training Procedure* (p. 9). SRI International. Retrieved on

March 15, 2018, from https://www.cia.gov/library/readingroom/docs/CIA-RDP96-00787R000300110001-8.pdf.

Kress. 1999. *Parapsychology in Intelligence: A Personal Review and Conclusions (UNCLASSIFIED)*. Retrieved on April 2, 2018, from http://citeseerx.ist.psu.edu/viewdoc/summary?doi=10.1.1.681.2907.

Laszlo, Ervin. 2004. *Science and the Akashic Field*, 2nd ed. Rochester, VT: Inner Traditions. 115.

LifeWay Research. 2014. *American Prayer Practices*. Nashville, TN: Lifeway Research. http://www.lifewayresearch.com/files/2014/09/American-Prayer-Practices.pdy and http://www.lifewayresearch.com/2014/10/01/americansprayforfriendsandfamily-2/.

Lumari. 2003. *Akashic Records: Collective Keepers of Divine Expression*. Santa Fe, NM: Amethyst. 23.

Newcombe, Rachel. n.d. "Pendulum Dowsing: An Introduction to Using a Pendulum." Received on February 23, 2019, from https://www.holisticshop.co.uk/articles/guide-pendulum-dowsing.

Newton, Michael. 2000. *Destiny of Souls: New Case Studies of Life Between Lives*. 24th printing, 2017. St. Paul, MN: Llewellyn Publications. 150.

Newton, Michael. 2009. *Memories of the Afterlife: Life Between Lives Stories of Personal Transformation*. Woodbury, MN: Llewellyn. Kindle Edition. 291.

Moody, Raymond. 2010. *Glimpses of Eternity: Sharing a Loved One's Passage from This Life to the Next*. Paradise Valley, AZ: SAKKARA Productions Publishing. 38.

Oakes, Luanne, PhD. 2006. *Sound Health, Sound Wealth: The Biology of Hope and Manifestation*. Nightingale-Conant. 59.

O'Neill, Jennifer. *Keys to the Spirit World: An Easy to Use Handbook for Contacting Your Spirit Guides.* Keys To The Spirit World LLC. Kindle Edition. 19.

Orr, Gabrielle. 2013. *Akashic Records.* San Bernardino, CA: Akashic Records. 31.

Ortiz, Ernesto. 2015. *The Akashic Records: Sacred Exploration of Your Soul's Journey within Wisdom of the Collective Consciousness.* Pompton Plains, NJ: New Page Books. 95.

Puthoff, Harold E., and Russell Targ. 1974. "Information Transmission under Conditions of Sensory Shielding." *Nature* 251 (5476): 602–7. *doi:10.1038/251602a0. PMID 4423858.* Retrieved on March 17, 2018, https://www.cia.gov/library/readingroom/docs/CIA-RDP96- 00787R000100220001-8.pdf.

PEW Research Center. *Frequency of Prayer.* Retrieved on March 6, 2018, from http://www.pewforum.org/religious-landscape-study/frequency-of-prayer/.

Richard Doland Show. 2019. "Russell Targ on the *Richard Dolan Show* plus 11-minute teaser *of Third Eye Spies.*" Retrieved on February 17, 2019, from https://www.youtube.com/watch?v=kqqcAJXtw00.

Ring, K., and E. E. Valarino. 1998. *Lessons from the Light: What We Can Learn from the Near- Death Experience.* New York: Insight Books. 154.

Shaked, Natan T., Barak Katz, and Joseph Rosen. 2009. *Review of Three-Dimensional Holographic Imaging by Multiple-Viewpoint-Projection Based Methods.* Appl. Opt. 48, H120- H136 (2009). https://www.osapublishing.org/ao/abstract.cfm?uri=ao-48-34-h120.

Shared Crossing Project. 2017. *Shared Death Experience.* Retrieved on April 3, 2018, from http://www.sharedcrossing.com/shared-death-experience.html.

Shaw, Patty, and Jacki Smith. 2013. *Do It Yourself Akashic Wisdom.* San Francisco, CA: Weiser Books. 202.

Silver, Tosha. 2015. *Change Me Prayers: The Hidden Power of Spiritual Surrender.* New York: Atria Books. 3.

Smith, Paul H. 2015. *The Essential Guide to Remote Viewing.* Cedar City, Utah: Intentional Press. 92–93.

Smithsonian. n.d. Chladni Plates. Retrieved on April 6, 2018, from http://americanhistory.si.edu/science/chladni.htm.

SparkNotes, eds. n.d. "SparkNote on Philosophical Investigations." Retrieved on March 17, 2018, from http://www.sparknotes.com/philosophy/investigations/.

Stearn, Jess. 1967. *Edgar Cayce: Sleeping Profit.* New York: Bantam Books.

Todeschi, Kevin J. 1998. *Edgar Cayce on the Akashic Records.* 22nd printing. Virginia Beach, VA: A.R.E. Press. 2.

Tomlison, Andy. 2007. *Exploring the Eternal Soul: Insights from the Life between Lives.* Dorset, UK: Heart Press. 62–63.

US Department of Health and Human Services. n.d. *Data and Statistics—DVT/PE-NCBDDD- CDC.* Retrieved on March 4, 2018, from https://www.cdc.gov/ncbddd/dvt/data.html/.

Van Praagh, James. 2017. *Wisdom from Your Spirit Guides: A Handbook to Contact Your Soul's Greatest Teachers.* Kindle Edition. Carlsbad: Hay House. 32, 38–39.

Vasudev, Sadhguru Jaggi. 2016. *Inner Engineering: A Yogi's Guide to Joy.* New York: Spiegel & Grau. 39.

Weiss, Brian. 2000. *Messages from the Masters: Tapping into the Power of Love.* New York: Grand Central Publishing. 188. Kindle Edition.

Wittgenstein, Ludwig. 1953. *Philosophical Investigations*, translated by G. E. M. Anscombe. Oxford: Basil Blackwell. Part I, section 242.

References by Chapter

Chapter 2

Abbott, Edwin A. May 25, 2012. *Flatland [illustrated]*. Art & Poetry Publishing. Kindle Edition.

De Tamble, Scott Fitzgerald. 2018. *Light Between Lives--Library and Life Selection*. Retrieved on March 25, 2018, from http://lightbetweenlives.com/about_lbl/library_life_selection.html.

Holden, J. M., B. Greyson, and D. James. 2009. *The Handbook of Near-Death Experiences: Thirty Years of Investigation*. Santa Barbara, CA: Praeger. 45–46, 229.

Laszlo, Ervin. 2004. *Science and the Akashic Field*. 2nd ed. Rochester, VT: Inner Traditions. 115.

Lumari. 2003. *Akashic Records: Collective Keepers of Divine Expression*. Santa Fe, NM: Amethyst. 23.

Ring, K., and E. E. Valarino. 1998. *Lessons from the Light: What We Can Learn from the Near- Death Experience*. New York: Insight Books. 154.

Shaked, Natan T., Barak Katz, and Joseph Rosen. 2009. *Review of Three-Dimensional Holographic Imaging by Multiple-Viewpoint-Projection Based Methods*. Appl. Opt. 48, H120- H136 (2009). https://www.osapublishing.org/ao/abstract.cfm?uri=ao-48-34-h120.

Tomlison, Andy. 2007. *Exploring the Eternal Soul: Insights from the Life between Lives*. Dorset, UK: Heart Press. 62–63.

Chapter 3

Hein, Simeon. 2010. "Learn Remote Viewing Step 1: The Cool Down." Retrieved on March 17, 2018, from https://www.youtube.com/watch?v=mMws4s8PBXg.

Hein, Simeon. 2010. "Learn Remote Viewing Step 2: Connecting with the Signal Line." Retrieved on March 17, 2018, from https://www.youtube.com/watch?v=TSf0UzG-scg.

Hein, Simeon. 2010. "Learn Remote Viewing Step 3: Tuning into the Target's Resonance." Retrieved on March 17, 2018, from https://www.youtube.com/watch?v=GDDunSxIRpk.

Hein, Simeon. 2010. "Learn Remote Viewing Step 4: Opening the Aperture." Retrieved on March 17, 2018, from https://www.youtube.com/watch?v=zBFDxp0emV0.

Hein, Simeon. 2010. "Learn Remote Viewing Step 5: Closing the Session." Retrieved on March 17, 2018, from https://www.youtube.com/watch?v=OfAStNZqJQ0&t=367s.

Hubbard, Scott G., and Gary O. Langford. 1986. *A Suggested Remote Viewing Training Procedure* (p. 9). SRI International. Retrieved on March 15, 2018, from https://www.cia.gov/library/readingroom/docs/CIA-RDP96-00787R000300110001-8.pdf.

Kress. 1999. *Parapsychology in Intelligence: A Personal Review and Conclusions (UNCLASSIFIED)*. Retrieved on April 2, 2018, from http://citeseerx.ist.psu.edu/viewdoc/summary?doi=10.1.1.681.2907.

Oakes, Luanne, PhD. 2006. *Sound Health, Sound Wealth: The Biology of Hope and Manifestation*. Nightingale-Conant. 59.

Orr, Gabrielle. 2013. *Akashic Records*. San Bernardino, CA: Akashic

Records. 31.

Puthoff, Harold E., and Russell Targ. 1974. "Information Transmission under Conditions of Sensory Shielding." *Nature* 251 (5476): 602–7. *doi:10.1038/251602a0. PMID 4423858.* Retrieved on March 17, 2018, from https://www.cia.gov/library/readingroom/docs/CIA-RDP96- 00787R000100220001-8.pdf.

Chapter 4

Cannon, Dolores. 2011. *The Three Waves of Volunteers and the New Earth.* Huntsville, AR: Ozark Mountain Publishing. 9–11.

Chapter 5

Braden, Gregg. 2000. *The Isaiah Effect: Decoding the Lost Science of Prayer and Prophecy.* New York: Three Rivers Press. 146–47.

Cannon, Dolores. 1993. *Between Death and Life: Newly Updated and Revised Edition.* 13th printing. Huntsville, AR: Ozark Mountain Publishing. 90.

Cannon, Dolores. 2011. *The Three Waves of Volunteers and the New Earth.* Huntsville, AR: Ozark Mountain Publishing. 9–11.

Chyan, Jiyuh. 2017. *Your Key to the Akashic Records.* McLean, VA: Difference Press. 21.

Howe, Linda. 2010. *How to Read the Akashic Records: Accessing the Archive of the Soul and Its Journey.* Boulder, CO: Sounds True. 11–12.

Newton, M. 2000. Destiny of Souls: New Case Studies of Life Between Lives. 24th printing, 2017. St. Paul, MN: Llewellyn Publications. 150.

Ortiz, Ernesto. 2015. *The Akashic Records: Sacred Exploration of*

Your Soul's Journey Within Wisdom of the Collective Consciousness. Pompton Plains, NJ: New Page Books. 26.

Stearn, Jess. 1967. *Edgar Cayce: Sleeping Profit.* New York: Bantam Books.

Todeschi, Kevin J. 1998. *Edgar Cayce on the Akashic Records.* 22nd printing. Virginia Beach, VA: A.R.E. Press. 2.

Chapter 7

Cannon, Dolores. 2011. *The Three Waves of Volunteers and the New Earth.* Huntsville, AR: Ozark Mountain Publishing. 9–11.

Chapter 8

Braden, Gregg. 2000. *The Isaiah Effect: Decoding the Lost Science of Prayer and Prophecy.* New York: Three Rivers Press. 146–47.

Howe, Linda. 2010. *How to Read the Akashic Records: Accessing the Archive of the Soul and Its Journey.* Boulder, CO: Sounds True. 11–12.

LifeWay Research. 2014. *American Prayer Practices.* Nashville, TN: Lifeway Research. http://www.lifewayresearch.com/files/2014/09/American-Prayer-Practices.pdy; http://www.lifewayresearch.com/2014/10/01/americansprayforfriendsandfamily-2/.

Ortiz, Ernesto. 2015. *The Akashic Records: Sacred Exploration of Your Soul's Journey Within Wisdom of the Collective Consciousness.* Pompton Plains, NJ: New Page Books. 95.

PEW Research Center. *Frequency of Prayer.* Retrieved on March 6, 2018, from http://www.pewforum.org/religious-landscape-study/frequency-of-prayer/.

Silver, Tosha. 2015. *Change Me Prayers: The Hidden Power of*

Spiritual Surrender. New York: Atria Books. 3.

Vasudev, Sadhguru Jaggi. 2016. *Inner Engineering: A Yogi's Guide to Joy*. New York: Spiegel & Grau. 39.

Chapter 10

Holden, J. M., B. Greyson, and D. James. 2009. *The Handbook of Near-Death Experiences: Thirty Years of Investigation*. Santa Barbara, CA: Praeger. 45–46.

Chapter 11

ADC Project. *After-Death Communications*. Retrieved on March 4, 2018, from http://www.after- death.com/.

De Tamble, Scott Fitzgerald. *Light Between Lives: The Loving Wisdom of Spirit*. Retrieved on March 1, 2018, from http://www. lightbetweenlives.com/about_lbl/spirit_guides.html.

Guggenheim, Bill, and Judy Guggenheim. 1995. *Hello from Heaven! A New Field of Research— After-Death-Communication—Confirms Life and Love are Eternal*. New York: Bantam Books.

Newton, Michael. 2009. *Memories of the Afterlife: Life Between Lives Stories of Personal Transformation*. Woodbury, MN: Llewellyn. 291. Kindle Edition.

O'Neill, Jennifer. *Keys to the Spirit World: An Easy to Use Handbook for Contacting Your Spirit Guides*. Keys To The Spirit World LLC. 19. Kindle Edition.

Ortiz, Ernesto. 2015. *The Akashic Records: Sacred Exploration of Your Soul's Journey within Wisdom of the Collective Consciousness*. Pompton Plains, NJ: New Page Books. 134–35.

Shaw, Patty, and Jacki Smith 2013. *Do It Yourself Akashic Wisdom*.

San Francisco, CA: Weiser Books. 202.

US Department of Health and Human Services. n.d. Data and Statistics—*DVT/PE-NCBDDD- CDC.* Retrieved on March 4, 2018, from https://www.cdc.gov/ncbddd/dvt/data.html/.

Van Praagh, James. 2017. *Wisdom from Your Spirit Guides: A Handbook to Contact Your Soul's Greatest Teachers.* Kindle Edition. Carlsbad: Hay House. 32, 38–39.

Weiss, Brian. 2000. *Messages from the Masters: Tapping into the Power of Love.* New York: Grand Central Publishing. 188. Kindle Edition.

Chapter 12

Abrams, Douglas, et al. 2016. *The Book of Joy.* New York: Avery. 145.

Chapter 13

Moody, Raymond. 2010. *Glimpses of Eternity: Sharing a Loved One's Passage from This Life to the Next.* Paradise Valley, AZ: SAKKARA Productions Publishing. 38.

Shared Crossing Project. 2017. *Shared Death Experience.* Retrieved on April 3, 2018, from http://www.sharedcrossing.com/shared-death-experience.html.

Smith, Paul H. 2015. *The Essential Guide to Remote Viewing.* Cedar City, Utah: Intentional Press. 92–93.

Smithsonian. n.d. Chladni Plates. Retrieved on April 6, 2018, from http://americanhistory.si.edu/science/chladni.htm.

SparkNotes, eds. n.d. *SparkNote on Philosophical Investigations.* Retrieved on March 17, 2018, from http://www.sparknotes.com/

philosophy/investigations/.

Wittgenstein, Ludwig. 1953. *Philosophical Investigations*, translated by G. E. M. Anscombe. Oxford: Basil Blackwell. Part I, section 242.

Chapter 16

Newcombe, Rachel. n.d. "Pendulum Dowsing: An Introduction to Using a Pendulum." Retrieved on February 23, 2019, from https://www.holisticshop.co.uk/articles/guide-pendulum-dowsing.

Richard Doland Show. 2019. "Russell Targ on the Richard Dolan Show plus 11-minute teaser of *Third Eye Spies*." Retrieved on February 17, 2019, from https://www.youtube.com/watch?v=kqqcAJXtw00.

Other References and Interesting Links

Information on healing with music:

http://www.songwritingwithsoldiers.org/

Information on Chladni Plates:

http://americanhistory.si.edu/science/chladni.htm
https://www.youtube.com/watch?v=tFAcYruShow

Flatland Video Dr. Carl Sagan:

https://www.youtube.com/watch?v=iiWKq57uAlk

Tuning Fork Video

https://www.youtube.com/watch?v=aCocQa2Bcuc)

Coventry Creations:

http://coventrycreations.com/

Contact Information for Scott Fitzgerald De Tamble, CHt

http://www.lightbetweenlives.com
http://www.lightbetweenlives.com/about_us/about_us_index.html

Remote Viewing

http://instituteforresonance.org/about

Paul Smith, Remote Viewing: Martial Art for the Mind https://www.youtube.com/watch?v=Z0yB_yUPiOc&t=588s Paul Smith, Remote Viewing FAQ. https://rviewer.com/faq-2/

Contact Information for Angela Thompson Smith, PhD

http://mindwiseconsulting.com/
http://mindwiseconsulting.com/?page_id=24

Associate Remote Viewing
https://vimeo.com/61851140

Acknowledgments

Thank you to all my family for being supportive as I continue my spiritual explorations. A special thank you to my wife and partner in life, Michelle, for continuing to encourage me to follow my passions. Thank you, babe, for sharing this great adventure with me. Thank you to my daughters, sons, grandchildren, and extended family for their loving support and encouragement to keep on writing. Thank you to my mother for sharing her amazing spiritual experience and allowing me to share it with readers.

Thank you to a wonderful spiritual teacher, remote viewer, writer, friend, and manuscript reviewer, Angela Thompson Smith, PhD (http://www.mindwiseconsulting.com). Thank you to a talented healer, hypnotherapist, friend, and manuscript reviewer, Scott Fitzgerald De Tamble, CHt (http://www.lightbetweenlives.com/).

Many continued thanks to Ernest Morrow, MDiv, CHT (http://www.ernestmorrow.com), and Jo'Ann Ruhl (http://www.joannruhl.com/) for continuing to encourage me to keep on listening to the silence and doing the work. Thank you to Cynthia Mun, Jenny Mackay, and all my friends at the Society of Children's Book Writers and Illustrators (SCBWI) who have been supportive and encouraging as I worked on many writing projects.

A special thank you to my editor, Debbie Upton. And a sincere thank you to Nancy Vernon, Brandy McDonald, and all of the hard-working folks at Ozark Mountain Publishing for all they do to bring amazing books to readers.

About the Author

When Rick isn't dreaming, you'll find him trying to discover why figuring out how, uncovering ancient mysteries, inventing something seriously cool, or learning something new.

Rick is a lifelong inventor and named inventor on over one hundred and twent patents. He has degrees in Avionics Systems Technology, Comupter Science and an MBA from Florida Institute of Technology. His experience includes a wide range of engineering, technology development and management roles ranging from space systems to gameing systems. He is a proud member of the Interneational Association for Near Death Studies, Society of Children's Book Writers and Illustrators (SCBWI) the Delta Mu Delta Honor Society, and hte Phi-Kappa Phi Honor Society.

http://www.richardrowebooks.com

Books by Richard Rowe

The Reincarnation Series
Voices; Whispers; Carmina's Musing
Published by: Tree Lovers Press

The Adventures of Jayden Banks and the Jameson Twins
Game On; Black Skulls; Spring Tide Mason Handbook
Published by: Tree Lovers Press

Changing the World One Invention at a Time
Published by: iUniverse

Imagining the Unimaginable
Published by Ozark Mountain Publishing

OZARK
MOUNTAIN
PUBLISHING

For more information about any of the above titles, soon to be released titles, or other items in our catalog, write, phone or visit our website:
Ozark Mountain Publishing, Inc.
PO Box 754, Huntsville, AR 72740
479-738-2348/800-935-0045
www.ozarkmt.com